MW01008833

UNLOVING
SPIRITS

HENRY W. WRIGHT

4178 Crest Highway
Thomaston, Georgia 30286

www.beinhealth.com

EAN   978-1-934680-13-1

Copyright Notice

© Copyright: 2007. Pleasant Valley Church, Inc.

All rights reserved. Any material, be it in written form, audio, video, compact disc, website postings – whether it be text, HTML, audio streaming or graphic images related to Pleasant Valley Church, Inc. or **Be in Health**™ may not be mirrored, reproduced, or displayed in whole or in part on another webpage or website (whatever the nature or purpose), or in any publication or collection of widespread circulation, whether offline or online (whatever the nature or purpose), even if considered "fair use," without express written permission from **Be in Health**™ or Pleasant Valley Church, Inc.

Disclaimer

This ministry does not seek to be in conflict with any medical or psychiatric practices nor do we seek to be in conflict with any church and its religious doctrines, beliefs or practices. We are not a part of medicine or psychology, yet we work to make them more effective, rather than working against them. We believe many human problems are fundamentally spiritual with associated physiological and psychological manifestations. This information is intended for your general knowledge only. Information is presented only to give insight into disease, its problems and its possible solutions in the area of disease eradication and prevention. It is not a substitute for medical advice or treatment for specific medical conditions or disorders. You should seek prompt medical care for any specific health issues. Treatment modalities around your specific health issues are between you and your physician.

As pastors, ministers and individuals of this ministry, we are not responsible for a person's disease, nor are we responsible for his or her healing. All we can do is share what we see about a problem. We are not professionals; we are not healers. We are only ministers ministering the Scriptures, and what they say about this subject, along with what the medical and scientific communities have also observed in line with this insight. There is no guarantee that any person will be healed or any disease be prevented. The fruit of this teaching will come forth out of the relationship between the person and God based on these insights given and applied. This ministry is patterned after the following scriptures: 2 Corinthians 5:18-20; 1 Corinthians 12; Ephesians 4; Mark 16:15-20.

Preface

This booklet was developed from a teaching to a live audience and has been kept in a conversational format. It is designed to reach a personal level with the reader rather than present a structured, theological presentation. Many times the reader will feel that Pastor Henry is talking directly to him or her. The frequent use of the pronoun *you* is meant to penetrate the human heart for conviction, not for accusation. Pastor Henry has been called to the office of pastor, and as such, he takes care of God's flock (whereas one called to the office of teacher does not take care of the sheep).

CONTENTS

UNLOVING SPIRITS

INTRODUCTION

If you stare at yourself in the mirror and do not like what you see, there is a good possibility you have an Unloving spirit. In order to gain freedom from Unloving, you must first deal with Bitterness, Envy and Jealousy and Rejection.

You have to love yourself, not get stuck on yourself. Knowing who God created you to be helps you to love yourself.

You MUST accept yourself.

You first have to deal with Rejection and self-rejection. You must deal with Rejection by others and forgive those who rejected you. You also have to forgive yourself. *Next to God, you ought to be your own best friend.* Yes, your best friend should be you, yourself. You should enjoy yourself. If you reject yourself, do you know what you are saying to God? "You made a mistake in creating me and you are a liar."

You may say, "Pastor, you don't know what my daddy told me when I was 6 or 13 or 28 or 49."

Do you know how many daddies and mommies are still oppressing their children when they are in their 20's and

30's, 40's and 50's? Tell those parents to get a life and get a grip. Say, "I am an adult; leave me alone!"

Do you know what happened to Job and his kids? They died because of Job's Fear. What Job feared the most came upon him.

> For the thing which I greatly feared is come upon me, and that which I was afraid of is come unto me. Job 3:25

DEFEATING UNLOVING SPIRITS

LEAVE FATHER AND MOTHER

To be free of an Unloving spirit, you are going to have to leave your father and mother. Move out of the house and stay out! I went through this in my life. I was oppressed. My father behaved like the devil in more ways than one, even though he was a minister. If you want to have some problems, have a man in your life, who is supposed to represent God, damage you and victimize you! It is a big stumbling block.

You may have had a father who was not saved and did not treat you right, but you can rationalize that and say, "Well, he was just goofy spiritually." When someone who is supposed to represent God to you treats you badly, it creates a breach that only God can heal. It's a miracle that I'm even standing here. I was rapidly going insane because of parental abuse and rejection.

The basis of all insanity is a breakdown in the family.

Physiologically, all insanity is a result of an over- or underproduction of various neurotransmitters, and this hyper- or hyposecretion is spiritually rooted.

2

Your enemy knows how to get to you, because he has made a study of you. It is time for a reality check. Your enemy knows you better than you know yourself, and he knows how to trip you up. He damaged your parents, he damaged your grandparents, and he is going to damage your children if you don't snap to it. It's time to wake up. It's time for a reality check.

Many times an Unloving spirit comes into you because you are a victim. The people who are victimizing you will tell you that it is all your fault, and that they would not be victimizing you if you had not been bad in a certain way. This happens in marriages, in families and in any relationship.

Romans ought to help you begin to unravel the Unloving spirit in your life.

> **Therefore thou art inexcusable, O man, whosoever thou art that judgest: for wherein thou judgest another, thou condemnest thyself; for thou that judgest doest the same things.** Romans 2:1

You must leave the spiritual dynamics of your family if you are of the years of understanding.

Leave mother and father because you have inherited things that are not of God.

So if you are going to be a spiritual man or woman in your own right, you must spiritually get away from the things that are not of God. It does not mean get away from your family; it means you must make the separation spiritually. No longer should you be a victim of your family iniquities that still want to become part of your thinking. This includes your married family tree; there are all kinds of dynamics that come into it.

Look at Job.

> ⁴And his sons went and feasted *in their* houses, every one his day, and sent and called for their three sisters to eat and to drink with them.
> ⁵And it was so, when the days of *their* feasting were gone about, that Job sent and sanctified them, and rose up early in the morning, and offered burnt offerings *according* to the number of them all: for Job said, It may be that my sons have sinned, and cursed God in their hearts. Thus did Job continually. Job 1:4-5

LET YOUR CHILDREN GO

Do you think Job had a little Fear? Many parents won't let their children go. I came to God seven years after my mother died, so she never saw the object of her faith. The Bible simply says about children,

> Train up a child in the way he should go: and when he is old, he will not depart from it. Proverbs 22:6

Many parents need their children for emotional support. Many parents are in child idolatry, making idols out of their children. Many parents, in the name of love, oppress and possess their children, and there is no way possible that God could raise their child. The Holy Spirit just sits back and says, "Well, I guess the parents are their Holy Spirit; they know better than God." The only thing the Bible says about parents and children is:

Teach your children the knowledge of God.

...and who they are is God's business.

God spoke to Jeremiah the prophet saying:

> ⁴Then the word of the LORD came unto me, saying,
> ⁵Before I formed thee in the belly I knew thee; and before thou camest forth out of the womb I sanctified thee, *and* I ordained thee a prophet unto the nations. Jeremiah 1:4-5

Who is in charge of Jeremiah's career, his parents or God? I can see his parents now, "A prophet?! Don't you understand, Jeremiah, they stone people like you?! There is no job security in being a prophet."

Later on when Jeremiah was being so oppressed by God's people, being put in stocks and bonds and thrown into prison, he even bemoaned the day he was born.

> **Cursed *be* the day wherein I was born: let not the day wherein my mother bare me be blessed.** Jeremiah 20:14

He cursed the day his mother conceived him, and in the midst of his Self-Pity, in his moaning and groaning, while he was being trashed by the very people who God was trying to save through him, he said, "But alas, I can't stop it because there is a fire that burns within me that can't be quenched. I have to speak for God."

> **Then I said, I will not make mention of him, nor speak any more in his name. But *his word* was in mine heart as a burning fire shut up in my bones, and I was weary with forbearing, and I could not *stay*.** Jeremiah 20:9

Wow! That will jerk the slack out of you! It was not Jeremiah's parents' decision who Jeremiah would be; it was God's decision.

I'll never forget one time when my father had this fixation that you only could be successful in life if you worked for the government. His goal was that I would work for the government because there was security and retirement. I coined this phrase in my own life, "Security is an illusion; there is nothing in life but opportunity." Insecurity is rooted in Fear and not trusting God. There is nothing wrong with planning for your future. The Bible is very clear about stewardship, but we are talking about Fear. I was probably 22 or 23 at the time, and I had gone to work for an insurance company as an underwriter in the home office of a mutual, underwriting fire insurance and automobile insurance.

If you do not work for the government, you work for an insurance company. So I started working at $75.00 a week as an underwriter, and in 40 years I might have been head of the mutual. Over a period of six months, I got a $10 raise to $85 a week. I was making $85 a week working my five hours a day, sitting behind a desk handling agent's calls and underwriting, writing risks for buildings for fire insurance and automobiles.

It was not an exciting life. Eventually I had everything done by 10:00 in the morning. A lady went on vacation, and I did all her work and was done by 11:00. Another person quit, and I did all their work and was done by 12:00. Then the rest of the afternoon I did crossword puzzles and waited for agent's calls. That was my life — not very exciting, but a very, very secure life.

Well, $85 a week is not a lot of money. I was restless and had a chance to go work for a company as a manufacturer's representative. This company made power actuated tools for shooting concrete nails and studs into wood, concrete or steel drilling systems. They were expanding in America. I went to work at $150 a week plus commission. I had a company vehicle and a full insurance program.

My father went through the ceiling and kicked me out, so I lost a place to stay. Because I left a cushy job at an insurance company, I had to go get my own apartment which cost me a little more money. I left $85 a week for $150 a week, plus a company vehicle and all expenses. I left a nice insurance group for an international company.

The best thing I ever did was leave that insurance company. Can you imagine me sitting behind a desk doing crossword puzzles from 1:00 until 5:00? Is that what God wanted me to do? But that was the object of my parent's intention.

Give your kids to God and stay out of their lives.

Love them, teach them the ways of God, stay out of their life and when they are old enough to go on their own, leave them alone! If they are blowing it, pray for them. If they come for assistance, give them advice, but it is still their choice. Do you know how many families are devastated in rage, anger, Bitterness and hurt because someone did not meet another's expectation? The child is now an adult!

Do you know how many parents that are 80 years old oppress their 60-year-old children? Do you know how many 80-year-old mothers and fathers treat their 60-year-old sons and daughters like they were 6 years old? That is sick! That is not godly; leave them alone! By interfering in their life, parents cause more trouble spiritually for their children than you can imagine.

When they become an adult, let them act like one. Do you know how many parents are still dependent on their children? Do you know how many families I deal with where the parents are the children, and the children are the adults? Do you know how many parents look to their children to be the spiritual leaders of their homes? We need to be taught the ways of God.

Many of you have Unloving spirits within you because you have not been released by your parents; you are oppressed. My father was an expert fisherman and hunter, and he was an expert carpenter and builder. He never once taught me how to fire a gun or how to fish; I never hunted in my life.

7

He would go off sometimes for a week at a time, way out at a hunting camp somewhere in the woods in the fall of the year; he would get two deer in Canada and one in Maine. I am an only child, a son, and not one time was I invited to go hunting, at least to tag along and have the joy of going in the woods. Not one time was I told how to handle a hammer or how to measure a board. What a loss of legacy.

Sometimes I think we need to pay more attention that we take the time to teach our children. Most of the time our children are oppressed by our ungodly spirituality, and our own hatred is extended to them. They become an object of our own spiritual problems.

Job had a problem. He was fretting over the spiritual condition of his children. He did not trust God for his children; Job had become a savior to his own children. He was not just praying for his children; he was worrying that they would offend God. Job lost all of his children to the devil.

God gave him back new children – more sons and daughters, but Job had some spiritual problems. In Job 40 and 41, we find that he had two principalities in his life – one was called Leviathan and one was called Behemoth. Leviathan is the father of the children of pride, and Behemoth is one who is chief in the knowledge of the ways of God. So when you are chief in the knowledge of the ways of God and you have pride, you have a real problem.

But Job also had another problem – he had a spirit of Fear. Not only that, but he had a personality of Fear. Job was worrying and carrying on about his children, and he would not release them to God. He did not trust God, and he paid a high price.

Job says,

> [24]For my sighing cometh before I eat, and my roarings are poured out like the waters.
> [25]For the thing which I greatly feared is come upon me, and that which I was afraid of is come unto me.   Job 3:24-25

Fear is an open door.

Fear demands to be fulfilled as an object of Satan's faith.

Faith and Fear are equal in the spiritual dimension. Both demand to be fulfilled.

When you dip into Fear, it demands that what you are afraid of be fulfilled. Faith demands to be fulfilled. "Faith is the substance of things hoped for, the evidence not yet seen." Fear is the substance of things not hoped for.

If you do not believe, if you have a Fear of loving yourself, you can forget about being delivered. If you are not prepared to accept yourself, that is a Fear. It negates God's faith for you. God is saying, "You are loved. I love you, and you are accepted. You are the apple of my eye. From the foundation of the world, I knew you would be here. I don't care what your mommy or daddy said to you. I don't care who cursed you with their tongue. You are mine."

When you are born again, you are God's. It does not make any difference what your mommy and daddy said to you ever again. It does not make any difference what your parents said to you; when you are born again, that is over with. Your Father is God. Jesus is your eternal husband forever in the mystical sense, and you belong to God. So you might as well settle this in your heart once and for all.

I listened to stuff in my life. Maybe you have listened to it in yours. I came to the conclusion it didn't really apply to me. It is amazing how people who are agreeing with evil spirits from their family trees will project things into their kids' lives and make them evil. Do you know how many grown-ups feel unclean and unworthy because their parents projected that into them, but they were not bad at all? Maybe you feel that today, but you were not bad at all.

Maybe you did not do anything wrong, maybe you were a good kid, maybe you had a good soft heart and they dumped their evil spiritual dynamics on you until you believed it was you. That is a lie! But when you do not cast it down as a lie, you establish it as a way of life for yourself.

To be free of unclean, Unloving spirits, you are going to have to repent to God.

Repent for carrying the torch of self-hatred.

You are not an extension of the sins of your parents, if you do not agree with them. Do you remember Ezekiel 18? It says the child shall not die for the sins of his parents, of his father. You do not have to die. They get passed on to you, but you can reject them. You do not have to die.

JOB'S EXAMPLE

So the thing which Job feared the most concerning his children came upon him. In Job, we will see an evil spirit present with Job.

> [12]Now a thing was secretly brought to me, and mine ear received a little thereof.
> [13]In thoughts from the visions of the night, when deep sleep falleth on men,
> [14]Fear came upon me, and trembling, which made all my bones to shake.
> [15]Then a spirit passed before my face; the hair of my flesh stood up:

> ¹⁶It stood still, but I could not discern the form thereof: an image *was* before mine eyes, *there was* silence, and I heard a voice, *saying*...   Job 4:12-16

Job had a spirit of Fear. One of his fears had to do with not releasing his children. You have to prepare yourself to leave your family spiritually in the areas where they are not right with God. You have to fall out of agreement with it. If they are not right with God and they made a victim of you spiritually, then you are now wearing that thing on the inside of you.

Don't listen to voices from the past.

You are going to have to fall out of agreement with it and prepare to walk away from it. You do not have to continue to hear the voices of your mother and father in your ears. If you do, it is an evil spirit that is tormenting you with self-rejection and self-hatred, and that is the Unloving spirit.

Are you still listening to the voices of parents who victimized you spiritually? There is no way I can take away those voices, but there is a way you can be free of the spirits that are tormenting you. That is the Unloving spirit. That is Rejection. That is self-hatred. That is what has stayed with you, but we are going to have a work of grace and mercy through God here.

You will always remember those voices. That is part of your memory, but you are not going to meditate on them anymore. Your memory is your memory, but the pain and the presence of those evil spirits that are attacking you and accusing you, when they are gone, you are going to have the memory, but you are not going to have the Accusation and the pain. You can stand there free.

I can remember right now, standing and hearing the voice of my father rejecting me, but I have no pain. I still feel

11

loved, and I am not in Rejection. I do not have an Unloving spirit, and I feel complete before God. I can hear every word, and it does not affect me whatsoever. I am not into denial, and I am not stuffing it. I am not going into alternate personalities to cope with it. It is just that I am free. I am free; it is not me.

When you think about it, if you are struggling with an Unloving spirit, you really are innocent, aren't you? You really were innocent from the beginning, weren't you? You were none of the things that you were accused of. You really were just a victim of their spirituality originating in the second heaven. That's why it hurts you so much. That's because the devil knew what he was doing.

You can unravel this, but you are going to have to want to be unraveled. There is no reason for you to go around in Rejection and self-rejection. This unclean, Unloving spirit that you have won't let you receive the love of others, even if they love you. It tells you that you are no good. That is a lie, because God has accepted you.

IDENTIFYING UNLOVING SPIRITS

An Unloving spirit attaches itself to you to make you feel rejected and reject yourself. It makes you feel unclean, unworthy and like you don't measure up. It makes you feel that you are no good. When you hear your voice talking, it is just like a piece of sandpaper on the side of a piece of metal. When you look at yourself in the mirror, the mirror says, "You old ugly thing." When you look at other people, you know they hate your guts because you see it in their eyes. (Well, maybe they hate themselves today, and you think they hate you.)

So you spend all your time debating with yourself as to whether you belong on this planet or not. Then you spend all your time moving the pieces around. You stand in front of the mirror and comb your hair this way. Yuck! You comb your hair that way. Yuck! You look at this wrinkle; you look at that sag. You look at those eyes - the same old eyes that stare at you every morning in the mirror. You say, "You are the ugliest thing I have ever seen."

You spend your day in a world of "not measuring up."

This person does not like me. That person does not like me. God does not like me. I do not even like myself. Why was I born?

Now if this person said "this" to me and that person said "that" to me... blah, blah, blah. You start replaying the same old message until the pages are worn, and it becomes your life. The evidence that an Unloving spirit has come to make its abode with you is that you are constantly struggling with yourself. That is its nature, and it needs you as a medium of expression.

When an Unloving spirit comes along and gets involved in your life, it's a parasite. It wants to go on stage. You are the puppet, and it is the hand that moves you. When we see you with an Unloving spirit, you are like a puppet going through the motions by the hand that someone or something else is making you say, do and think.

Are you constantly struggling with yourself?

It is time for you to be you. Tell that Unloving spirit that you do not need it. You can stand on the stage of life yourself. It is time for you to take back your identity. If someone doesn't like you, so what? God loves you, and there is no one greater than Him.

13

If someone says, "I don't like you," then you say, "My Father loves me." "Well, who is your Father?" "God. If your Father were God, then you would love me because I am your brother (your sister). If you do not love me and you are putting me down, then the love of God is not in you. He is not your Father; your father is the devil." Now if we say this face-to-face to people who reject us, we might have a chance at winning this one.

If people rise up against you, they too are a puppet of an Unloving spirit. When this happens, because you are in Self-Rejection and have an Unloving spirit, you withdraw in Fear of rejection. You withdraw in Fear of abandonment. You withdraw in Fear of man. You withdraw in Fear of failure, and you go hide behind a rock. You say, "They're right."

No, they are not. Romans says,

> **God forbid: yea, let God be true, but every man a liar...**
> Romans 3:4

You are the apple of God's eye.

> **He found him in a desert land, and in the waste howling wilderness; he led him about, he instructed him, he kept him as the apple of his eye.** Deuteronomy 32:10

Do you want to continue to hate yourself? Are you about ready to take your place on this turf called earth in the name of Jesus, and get on with your life? You're going to have to come to the place where you stop fighting with yourself. Be aware that there are parts of you that will shut down and want to shut you down in the midst of this understanding.

There will be something in you that will want to scratch my eyes out, because this is one of the greatest bondages known to mankind: self-rejection, self-hatred, Fear of man and having an Unloving spirit. You have Fear of man, but the Word says that you should not Fear not what man can do to you, but put your trust in the Lord.

> So that we may boldly say, The Lord *is* my helper, and I will not fear what man shall do unto me.   Hebrews 13:6

REJECTION BEGAN IN YOUR OWN FAMILY

You need to leave home spiritually once and for all. Deuteronomy 32:10 tells of God's finding Jacob and His tender care for him. "He found him in a desert land and in the waste howling wilderness."

> He found him in a desert land, and in the waste howling wilderness; he led him about, he instructed him, he kept him as the apple of his eye.   Deuteronomy 32:10

They were wasted and separated from God. He led him about, He instructed him, and He kept him as the apple of His eye. In the *Dake* Bible, the notes say that word "apple" is the Hebrew word *iyshown,* which means the dark pupil of the eye, the hole, the gate, the door of the eye. The book of Psalms also refers to the apple of the eye.

> 7Shew thy marvellous lovingkindness, O thou that savest by thy right hand them which put their trust *in thee* from those that rise up *against them.*
> 8Keep me as the apple of the eye, hide me under the shadow of thy wings,   Psalm 17:7-8

What a statement to help you with Rejection! You have an Unloving spirit because you have been rejected, usually beginning in your own families. Rejected. The Lord is going to keep you from those that rise up against you. Psalm 17:8 says, "Keep me as the apple of your eye." The word Hebrew here, *iyshown,* means the little man of the eye. It is an idiom meaning "what is dearest to us" and "that which must have extreme care and protection."

The eyes of the Lord are over the righteous.

> The eyes of the LORD *are* upon the righteous, and his ears
> *are open* unto their cry.   Psalm 34:15

First Peter says,

> For the eyes of the Lord are over the righteous, and his
> ears are *open* unto their prayers: but the face of the Lord *is*
> against them that do evil.   1 Peter 3:12

In the Hebrew language when it says you are the apple of His eye, the very focus of His attention is right on you. You do not see out of the whites of your eyes.

If you have an Unloving spirit,
you cannot look another person in the eye.

People who have an Unloving spirit cannot look in the pupil of another person's eye for very long, because they get nervous and jerky. That is why I say, "Look at your neighbor, look in his beady little eyes and tell him, 'You are the best thing since peanut butter.' "

What am I doing? I am forcing that Unloving spirit to stand aside, so you can get into a place of fellowship in spite of it. You must be able to look at people in their eyes. If you are uncomfortable when someone looks into your eyes and starts to penetrate you with his eyes, you may have an Unloving, unclean spirit.

When you go up to people and say, "Good morning, how are you?" and they stiffen, that is a spirit of Rejection in them. But if they say, "Hi, give me a big hug," it does not mean we are strange. It means we are normal, just brothers in the Lord.

The Bible says,

Greet one another with an holy kiss.   2 Corinthians 13:12

YOU MUST BE IN FELLOWSHIP

That is the Word, but if you have an unclean, Unloving spirit, you will make our brotherly greeting evil because that thing hates fellowship. Perfect love casts out Fear.

There is no fear in love; but perfect love casteth out fear: because fear hath torment. He that feareth is not made perfect in love.   1 John 4:18

If you are going to have an Unloving spirit driven from you, you have to get into fellowship. If you see this person coming in Christ and you know they are going to say, "Hello how are you? Are you having a good day? I am going to give you a hug," don't avoid them.

To get rid of an Unloving spirit, you must be in fellowship with others.

When I came to the Lord, I had Rejection, Fear and an Unloving, unclean spirit. I was in a very large church. If you want to get lost as a Christian, find a big church of 1,000 people so no one will notice you. You can worship God in your silence and your isolation. There are people who get lost in crowds for that reason.

There was an elder in the church named Ron, and when he would see me, he would get me in a hug and not let me go. I would squirm and stiffen up. He would not just give me a hug; he would not let me go. What was in me? I had an Unloving, unclean spirit, and the more I would squirm, the more he would hold me. It's a wonder I did not leave that church. I would come into the service, and he would see me and say, "Come here."

17

I would go find another entrance to get away from this guy. This went on for months. Perfect love casts out Fear. One day I walked in, and he was right in my face. "Good morning brother, sure love ya."

Oh no, not again! I thought I had this all worked out. He took me in his arms, and he started that same old garbage all over again: just holding me and loving on me and sucking me into his belly. I mean just absorbing me into himself. All of a sudden it broke, and I went limp and just let him love me. When he was finished, I looked at him and said, "Now it is my turn." I took him in my arms and started loving him back and telling him how much I respected him and loved him. And it was over with. Then he was probably looking for a way to get away from me. That broke years of Rejection. One man loving correctly broke that reality.

He is also the same man that came up to me one day and said, "You are in sin." The Lord had started to use me in prophecy, and I was so afraid that I would be in divination that I would sit there, and my knuckles would get white holding onto that chair.

In that church you did not get up in the flesh too often, because that pastor would tell you to sit down. You had to wait to be acknowledged to come up and take the microphone because it was a large church, and the pastor wanted everyone to be edified when God spoke through the spirit of prophecy. So you had to stand and wait to be acknowledged before you could walk to the front. Fifteen hundred people made it a long walk to the front. You would walk down and look at the pastor and say, "I have a word."

He would stare at you, testing the spirits, then either gesture "no" or say, "Okay." Some nights he would gesture "no," and the person would walk back to his seat and sit down. That never happened to me, thank God. I never was

18

told to sit down, and I never was told, "I'll see you in my office Monday morning."

I survived it, but I would check the Spirit of God to the point that I was in sin because I did not want an evil spirit to speak through me in divination or false prophecy. I would check it and check it. I would just rock under it, and then sometimes I would disobey. Someone else would pop up and come down and say the very same word that was blowing through me. Boy, you talk about some guilt then. The devil used that big time.

One day the same guy that used to hold me (you know, my bosom buddy) came and stood in front of me. He was not smiling, and he did not hold me. He said, "Brother, I need a word with you." The Bible says,

> **Open rebuke *is* better than secret love.**   Proverbs 27:5

He loved me enough to speak for God and tell me the truth. Sometimes when I come around and tell you the truth, it is hard because of the Unloving spirits. It is hard sometimes for me as a pastor to be honest with you and tell you just like it is because sometimes you have so much Rejection and so many Unloving spirits within you, that you would take it as victimization. You would think I was mad at you because I did not smile at you when I pierced you with my eyes and said, "I need to have a word with you."

When I deal with my children, they are not bastards, they are children. The Bible says that if you love your children, you will instruct them and chasten them properly, not in an ungodly evil way, because the Bible says evil is bound up in the heart of a child from birth.

> **Foolishness *is* bound in the heart of a child; *but* the rod of correction shall drive it far from him.**   Proverbs 22:15

They inherited it from you. So if you tell them to get a grip while you go your merry way, they look at you and say, "Uh huh!" They are not deceived, you are.

So this guy came up to me and he said, "Brother you are in sin." Boy, you talk about doing your dirty laundry checklist real fast. He said, "You are in sin."

I said, "How?"

He said, "You've been quenching the Spirit of God. God has given you the spirit of prophecy, and you are not using it. If you do not come to grips with this thing, the Spirit of God will remove from you until you do." He said God had called me to be a prophet to the church and "If you do not start exercising your gifts at this level, you can forget about Him using you at that level."

It was still six months before I prophesied again. I was shaking in my boots because I did not want a devil to prophesy through me. Do you understand where I am coming from? The same man that loved me and broke the Unloving spirit, is the same man that came to me in the Spirit of the Lord and rebuked me. For whose benefit? Mine. I am a better man for it. An open rebuke is better than secret love.

REPENT SO GOD CAN DEAL WITH YOU

If you have an Unloving spirit that has not been removed, God cannot deal with you as children, and as a leader, I cannot deal with you representing the love of the Father and the love of the Lord. You will not be able to receive the chastening of the Lord, and you will not be able to receive instruction from God correctly. So God withdraws. Then we deal with you from a distance, until we can get to a point where you are able to receive the love of the Father at the level which will change things for you.

An Unloving spirit will keep you from being changed.

It will interfere with everything that God has for you. Why? Because just as Bitterness or unforgiveness will keep you from forgiveness of sin in your own life, an Unloving, unclean spirit will separate you from the love of God. Mark 11:26 says that if you from your heart do not forgive your brother his trespass, your Father which is in heaven shall not forgive you yours.

You need to be forgiven of your sins, or you will be separated from the love of God. If you are separated from the love of God, you cannot possibly love yourself, and it's impossible for you to receive or love your neighbor. You can't love your neighbor if you do not love yourself. You can't accept your neighbor unless you accept yourself. The spiritual dynamics are in place that will keep you from walking in the fulfillment and the freedom of that reality.

This has nothing to do with your feelings, because those feelings may be the nature of Satan manifesting through you as an Unloving spirit of self-hatred and Rejection and guilt. You have to identify that part of you that is not of God and make it your enemy. Those feelings when you cannot look someone in the eye, those feelings when you withdraw in Fear, those feelings that come when someone says you are beautiful and you think, "No I am not," those feelings that are within you that constantly accuse you to yourself, those feelings are your enemy because they are not from God, and they are not even from you.

They are the voices and the presence of the Unloving, unclean spirit and every spirit that answers to them, and

21

they have invaded your spirit, have invaded your soul, and have become part of your nature. You are now the puppet on the end of a hand.

Editor's Note: The teachings on *Separation*, available in the BE iN HEALTh™ bookstore, are highly recommended.

There came a place in my life when I got tired of being a puppet on the end of a foreign hand. I saw who I was in Christ. I saw that I was loved. I saw also that I had not arrived. I saw that I had areas in my life that were not pleasing to God.

But He is a loving Father and I read in 1 John that if I confessed my sins, He was faithful and just to forgive me my sins and to cleanse me from all unrighteousness.

If we confess our sins, he is faithful and just to forgive us
***our* sins, and to cleanse us from all unrighteousness.**
1 John 1:9

In the act of the relationship with God, I learned to come to Him in my unloveliness, in my Fear, in my torment, in every part of Rejection that I had, I learned to come before my Father and say:

"This is not me,
and it is separating me from Your love."

My relationship with God the Father is something that I have, and I am not going to let any Unloving, unclean spirit steal my relationship, ever! I do not care if *you* reject me, He has not. I do not care if anyone rejects you, the Father has not rejected you, and you have to settle that. If you do not settle that issue, you are continuing to make the devil your father.

UNIQUE IN THE BODY OF CHRIST

You are unique, you have unique characteristics, and you have pluses and minuses. The minuses that you have (or the pluses that someone else has) are not the whole picture: together we make up the composite body of Christ in the earth, and the fullness of God is manifest through all of us. You have to be who God created you to be. You do not have to be a clone of me.

We need each other. I would not be complete without you, without having known you and God's will for your life and seeing the beauty of the work of the Holy Spirit in you. To lose that, as a part of me forever, would be a tragedy.

I am jealous for your safety and jealous for your well-being because He is jealous for you. You are the apple of His eye, meaning you are the focus of His attention. God the Father in heaven loves you independently and individually, not collectively first. He loves you personally and individually. Then collectively, you are given to Christ as a gift.

Jesus did not come to show Himself to us; He came to show us the Father. After we have made our peace with God, then God the Father, as a work of the Holy Spirit, says now, "Jesus, look what I have for you. They are your bride forever. Aren't they beautiful?"

Jesus says, "It was worth the cross to get them." The first thing Jesus did in his death, was go into Paradise and bring all those people waiting for Him from Paradise in the bowels of the earth up to the third heaven to await resurrection. He went in and said, "Okay gang, here I am." I can see Him coming up to Abraham, "Abraham, thanks for holding out in your faith. I am here to get your fruit and you too." That is the love of God. You are not expendable.

23

I can feel the Spirit of God so strong, dealing with your heart. Father, I ask that the Spirit of God be released to start clobbering that Unloving spirit. You are not expendable. You say,

"It is not like the planet couldn't go on without me. I mean after all, I am not very significant. Mankind could do well without me; after all, everyone has told me that all my life. My daddy says that he wishes I had never been born. My momma said, 'Well I did not want you. You interfered with my sex life. I wanted to have a good time for five years, but now I have you, and I can't party like I used to. Now I have to stay home and take care of you. Besides I wanted a boy anyway.' "

All that stuff will scar you and make you feel unlovely. It is time you understand that in the new birth you became a new creature, and that old world is gone. It has passed. Behold all things have become new.

You have to believe that. You have to get hold of it, you have to accept it, and you have to realize and say to yourself before God, "I am not expendable." I want you to find someone next to you, and I want you to look at them right in the eye and say:

"You know what? I am not expendable in creation. God saved me because I am important. I am not going to listen to lies anymore. I do not care what my ancestors told me. They had an Unloving spirit too. That was their problem; I am going on with my life in the name of Jesus. Amen? Amen."

You have to get this into your heart.

PRAYER

I take authority over the devil that is ruling your spirit and your soul this day. I take authority over Satan and his kingdom today. I release your spirit to the love of God. I release your mind to the peace of the everlasting God for you. You are the apple of His eye. You are the object of His attention. He loves you with an everlasting love, and He came down in the form of Jesus Christ the Word, and He died a horrible, agonizing death just to save you. That is because of love. No greater love is there than a man who would lay his life down for another.

RENOUNCING

If you can't receive that, you have an Unloving, unclean spirit that needs to go. When you look in the mirror and you cannot say, "I am the righteousness of God in Christ Jesus by faith," that mirror is screaming at you that you are the ugliest thing that ever showed up today behind this bathroom sink. So you must look that thing straight in the eye and say:

"I *am* the apple of God's eye, and I am not who I *shall* be. In the twinkling of an eye I *shall* be changed and corruption *shall* put on incorruption, and mortality *shall* put on immortality. I am not as I *shall* be, but in the twinkling of an eye, I *shall* be changed. So Unloving spirit, leave."

Maybe it is time you become aggressive in reclaiming your life and tell the passivity of uncleanness and unloveliness and Rejection to hit the door of your life and not come back. If you want to cohabit with it, it will love to cohabit with you. But you are in charge, not it. You have been the tail, it has been the dog, and you are being wagged. I think it needs to go the other way. It is the tail that gets

25

wagged, and you are in control and in charge of your life in Christ Jesus, as the will of the Father.

You are the apple of His eye. First Peter says,

> For the eyes of the Lord *are* over the righteous, and his ears *are open* unto their prayers: but the face of the Lord *is* against them that do evil.   1 Peter 3:12

You are the object of God's love. You are the apple of His eye, and He gave the law, or the Word, to you for discernment. The book of Proverbs says,

> ²Keep my commandments, and live; and my law as the apple of thine eye. ³Bind them upon thy fingers, write them upon the table of thine heart. ⁴Say unto wisdom, Thou *art* my sister; and call understanding *thy* kinswoman.
> Proverbs 7:2-4

You are the fruit of Abraham, Isaac and Jacob; you are the fruit of their faith. God called him out of the desert. He has called you out of the desert and if you are by the faith of Abraham, by faith through Jesus Christ all the way down, then you are the apple of God's eye, and God has called you out of the desert of life because He loves you! If I could crawl inside you right now and just shout at you 24 hours a day, "You are loved! You are loved! You are loved! Receive the love!" I would scream in you for the rest of your life until you finally said, "Okay I get the picture. Enough, I accept it."

RESTORATION AND HEALING OF DISEASE

You must come to a place of perfect peace in three dimensions. The first dimension of peace you need is with the *Father* according to truth — not feeling, not religion, not emotion, but truth. You need peace in your doctrines of God, not what man has said. Secondly, you need perfect peace in your relationship with *yourself*. Unloving spirits in you keep you from peace with yourself. Thirdly, you need perfect peace with *others,* regardless of their mentalities or spiritualities.

You have not been taught to love yourself, but you have been taught to hate yourself. If someone did not tell you that you were lovely and wanted, they abused you to the point that you finally believed it anyway. The thing about it is that once that happens, you are programmed to abuse as you have been abused. There is your rollover in incest and your rollover in molestation. It is time this thing stops in your life. It is time for you to stop being tormented by the Unloving spirits that were in your ancestors and that are in you. It is time for you to stop being antichrist yourself and begin to tell the devil and his kingdom you are not going to listen to lies anymore.

What did God say about you in creation? You are the apple of His eye. Psalm 139 says you are fearfully and wonderfully made. You are the real queen of heaven; it is not Mary, it is not Ashteroth. You are the queen of heaven because you are the bride of Christ. God loves you no matter what your parents said or did to you.

If you cannot believe it and receive it, then you have an antichrist spirit because you are telling God He is a liar, and you are going to believe the lies of the devil before you believe the living God who has spoken to you from His Word. When are you going to mix it with your faith? Let God be true and every man a liar!

If you do not love yourself, you have an antichrist spirit.

If your parents trashed you in your childhood or your adulthood, they have an antichrist spirit. God comes first, not your mother and father; you belong to God. The parents' responsibility is to raise the children in the nurture and admonition of the Lord, to teach them the ways of the Lord, to teach them about God and to teach them that they belong to God, and that they will be His sons and daughters forever.

As a parent, all you are going to do is give that child back to God and be there to represent God to that child. Any parent that does not represent God the Father and God the Word and God the Holy Spirit on every perfect level to that child has an antichrist spirit within them. Otherwise they would obey God and take care of the children in godliness.

THE FIRST MINISTRY OF GOD

If you are over 18, then you are adults before God and no longer children. Leave your mother and your father once and for all and get on with being the sons and daughters of God in your own right. Your unclean, Unloving spirits of self-rejection and hatred need to be so miserable that they squirm and say, "I have had enough of this person. I am out of here; I'll go find someone else to inhabit that is less trouble."

**Be so filled up with God
that the devil is squeezed right out of you.**

In understanding who you are and that now you are an adult before God, you stand alone before Him. The first ministry of God, pure religion undefiled, is this: that you take care of the fatherless, you visit the widows and you keep yourself unspotted from the world.

> **Pure religion and undefiled before God and the Father is
> this, To visit the fatherless and widows in their affliction,
> *and* to keep himself unspotted from the world.**   James 1:27

That is the nuts and bolts of religion. Anything else other than that is just "stuff." The first ministry of God is to the fatherless and the widow from the standpoint of both biological death and spiritual separation.

Your father may be alive, but you are fatherless. If you are a female, your husband may be alive, but you are a spiritual widow. The first ministry of your Father in heaven is to you in this dimension, whether you are fatherless through biological death or spiritual separation. God's first ministry is to come through Jesus Christ and fill you up and fill that void and take away that Rejection. I do not care who your father is. I do not care who your mother is. I do not care who your husband is. I do not care who your wife is. If you are a man, you may be a spiritual widower as a husband. You may have been abandoned by a wife; you may have had a marriage that failed because of the evil one. God's first ministry is to restore you personally, in spite of your wife.

We are all going into eternity, and there are no mothers and fathers there for you. There are no husbands and wives there for you; you will be spiritually mature forever as the wife of Christ forever, in the mystical sense. So why dwell on this stuff any longer? He has delivered you. He has brought you out of it, so why dwell on it? Do not cry over spilt milk. Do not go back into hindsight. Do not go back in the past and live in the past, because *the devil wants to take your past and make it your future.*

The devil wants to take your past and make it your future.

Tell him to stay in the past; you are going on without him. You can leave mother and father and all of their hell behind. Do not drag junk into your children, because that is how the inherited curse comes in the rollover.

Thou shalt love the Lord thy God with all of thy heart. It does not say that you shall *obey* the Lord thy God.

> Jesus said unto him, Thou shalt love the Lord thy God with all thy heart, and with all thy soul, and with all thy mind. Matthew 22:37

Jesus said,

> If ye love me, keep my commandments. John 14:15

It does not say if you obey my commandments, I'll love you. God is going to love you whether you obey His commandments or not. For God so loved the world that He gave His only begotten Son...

> For God so loved the world, that he gave his only begotten Son, that whosoever believeth in him should not perish, but have everlasting life. John 3:16

In your life as a child, if you obeyed the law of the mother or father, whether it was righteous or unrighteous, then they would love you, right? No, you needed to receive love whether you obeyed them or not. Love has nothing to do with your disobedience; love is unconditional, constant, standard, moving straight ahead. If receiving love from your parents was conditional to you behaving or not behaving, they blew it.

I instruct my children firmly in righteousness and discipline, but I also cover it with love. They know they are loved in their disobedience as well as their obedience.

In correcting my young daughter once when she would not follow the law of her father, I had to stop her in her tracks and deal with it. It was a rod of correction verbally by discussion between us. Getting a two-year-old in dialogue is interesting. But she was fully alert and I said, "Now do you know that I love you?"

She said, "Yes, Daddy love me."

"Are you sure you know I love you?"

30

"Yes, Dad, I know you love me."

"You know I have to deal with you, right?"

"Yes, Dad, deal with me."

You just want to melt. You do not want to discipline anymore; you don't care anymore. You just want to go be a rebel because she just melted your heart. I was trying to get her attention and said, "If you do not stop, I am going to make you count to 100." She was two years old. I said, "Now, one." She said, "1." "Two." She said, "2." "Three." She said, "3." "Four." She said, "4." "Five." She said, "5." "Six." She said, "6." "Seven." She said, "7." "Eight." "8." "Nine." "9." "Ten." "10." "One hundred." "100." That was my grace and mercy!

"Do you know I love you?"

"Yes, Dad."

"You got a grip now?"

"Yes, sir!" Well, in two minutes she was up in my lap, hugging me and loving all over me, but it was broken. Love is not dependent on our obedience or disobedience. Love is our nature because that is the nature of our Father, and He loved the disobedient.

DOUBLE MINDEDNESS - REBELLION

Have you ever been rebellious against your parents or disagree with them about anything? Have you ever sassed your parents? Of course you have. In your heart you did; maybe you did not dare say it out loud.

Here is the love of God. In the book of Psalms there is a statement about Jesus that is fulfilled in Ephesians 4. "Thou hast ascended on high. Thou hast led captivity captive. Thou hast received gifts for men."

31

> **Thou hast ascended on high, thou hast led captivity captive: thou hast received gifts for men; yea, for the rebellious also, that the LORD God might dwell** *among them.*
>
> Psalm 68:18

The Lord wants to give you gifts, also for the rebellious, that the Lord God might dwell amongst you. God loves you even in your rebellion. He loves you even when you are goofy, but your parents did not always love you when you were goofy. Sometimes they were goofier than you, and they made you goofy; then they asked you to behave while they continued to misbehave. Now you wonder why you are in confusion, and you have schizophrenia to deal with.

The confusion of a double minded parent in the family is what produces schizophrenia. The kid goes "tilt," and we have an oversecretion of serotonin and an oversecretion of norepinephrine because life does not make any sense. "Wait a minute, I am supposed to be loved. What do you mean I have to behave, and you do not have to behave, parent? What do you mean, 'do as I say, not as I do?' What do you mean you are dropping me off at church, and you are not coming? What do you mean, I need to know Jesus, and you use His name in vain? What are you talking about, parent? Why are you telling me to 'love my brother' when you are beating momma up?" These are the scars of Satan. Let me tell you something. God loves you. He loves you even if you are a rebel.

I rebelled for years, in a nice way. I was a nice rebel. I didn't do anything dangerous. I was just in rebellion. In Rejection, Fear and rebellion, God loved me. That is why I love Him, and I accept His love. The Unloving spirit comes and says, "Well, yeah, the white's getting whiter in your beard, Pastor. Did you ever look at your yearbook when you were 18 and see the difference? Did you? Did you? Did you?" That is the voice of an Unloving spirit wanting to steal who you are.

Let me tell you something. Who you are is not the house you are living in anyway. It is not the house you live in. Some of you have rafters, some of you have thatched roofs, some of you have window panes, and some of you have little beady eyes that stare out of wood. Some of you are dressed up in different colors, but that is not you.

It is who you are inside - the spirit man on the inside is the real you. That is who got saved first. Your pour old soul has been getting fixed little by little as you go along. When you became born again, your spirit came alive to God and you made God the Father, "Abba *my* Father." You have to leave mother and father, and mother and father have to leave their children alone, whether they are bad or good. If the children need help, they can come back to mommy and daddy for counsel, but mommy and daddy need to mind their own business and pray for their children.

Romans 2 will help you understand the dynamics of the insanity of transference of spirits from parents into children. Your parents were not spiritual to you or for you. This will help unravel the confusion you might have, because when you are a child you do not know your parents are evil. It is a shock to find out. "What?! Mommy and daddy are evil and have done evil things to me?"

That scarring is something that breaches trust. When you do not trust people, it is impossible for you to love them in the natural, but it is not spiritually impossible to love them with God. In the natural, it is impossible to love people if you do not respect them.

"You make me feel bad. If it were not for you, I would not feel bad. You are the problem I am having a bad day because you are in my face."

"Well, Daddy, I am just standing here listening."

"Get out of my way. You are in my face."

HUSBANDS AND FATHERS

The salvation of mankind begins with the salvation of the husbands and the fathers.

The salvation of mankind begins with the salvation of the husbands and the fathers. The men need to get saved. If the men would get saved, the wives and the children would live in safety, and then our daughters could marry spiritually correct men. If the men are correct spiritually, the family can also be handled in a spiritually correct manner. That's the way it is. God intended that men be responsible for the safety, the teaching, the spirituality, the welfare and everything that is important for the wife and the children. I have not found one woman yet that does not have a desire to follow a godly man, unless she was so victimized about herself that she can't accept that kind of love.

Women are designed by God to follow a godly leader.

MEN SHOULD REPRESENT THE FATHER

God intended the man to be in charge to represent Him as Father and to be to the wife, as Christ is to the church. Any violation of that produces an Unloving spirit.

We have to get past this Fear and get into your heart. We have to get God in there so He can start to love on you and get you feeling all good on the inside. But now comes the finger of Accusation.

> [8]Finally, *be ye* all of one mind, having compassion one of another, love as brethren, *be* pitiful, *be* courteous:
> [9]Not rendering evil for evil, or railing for railing: but contrariwise blessing; knowing that ye are thereunto called, that ye should inherit a blessing.
> [10]For he that will love life, and see good days, let him refrain his tongue from evil, and his lips that they speak no guile:
>   1 Peter 3:8-10

This is not giving railing for railing, or verbal abuse for verbal abuse. "Railing for railing" means not playing spiritual ping-pong with your mouth. Do not repay evil for evil. The Bible says if you can't say anything good, do not say anything at all. Now here comes the spirit in the other person. Are you holding your peace? Are you gritting your spiritual teeth? You are taking this avalanche of verbal abuse in the name of Jesus and holding your peace. You stand there because you know the Word says anything less or more than that is evil. The person knows you are not responding, because he wants to use your words to shove them back down your throat. So he says to you, "You wimpy chicken you, you can't defend yourself. What do you have to say for yourself? Why are you standing there in silence? Respond to me."

That is a spirit in him goading you into that ping-pong, railing for railing, and it is banking on the fact that you have Rejection and an Unloving spirit which can get you all stirred up. Now we have that kind of war in the heavenlies and both people are victims.

REFUSE THE INIQUITIES OF YOUR ANCESTORS

Let's understand this spiritually. In order for you to be free of an Unloving spirit that came into you from Rejection by mother and father, or husband or wife, or brother or sister, or whoever, you are going to have to understand that what people accuse you of, they are themselves. You are not guilty. Well, you may have contributed to it, and if you have, then you are just like them.

But you are the spiritual one here today, and you can recover yourself. Who needs to get spiritual first, someone else or you? If we are going to unravel this mess, who would you suggest it begin with? You personally! But when you have an Unloving spirit, you also have Rejection and Bitterness. You say in your mind, "If they will come to me and take responsibility, then I'll respond. If *they* will just take responsibility, if *they* would just get it right."

Spiritually incorrect people cannot do spiritually correct things.

That is coming out of your need. That is coming out of your own Rejection. That is coming out of your need to be loved, but it is an inordinate affection. It is an inordinate love because it is not based out of giving; it is based out of receiving, and your completeness is now on the basis of receiving, not on who you are.

Who you are in love can be complete, and you do not need to receive it from anyone. If who you are is dependent on someone being nice to you, you have blown it already. You should be complete in yourself and in God, and then out of that strength you give unto others.

You say, "Well, if people would love me, then I would love them. If someone would love me, then I would love God."

No, you *love God first*, you love yourself second, and everything else will fall into place. If you do not apply these principles, they will never work. They are from the Scriptures, from the very throne of God, to help you recover yourself from the snare of the devil, to bring you to a place of understanding, of discernment and to a place of focus.

The Bible says you are working out your own salvation daily. You have to grab hold of these principles. You have to make up your mind that the Unloving spirit of Rejection and the stuff within you have to go. You are going to have to boot them out.

Romans says,

> Therefore thou art inexcusable, O man, whosoever thou art that judgest: for wherein thou judgest another, thou condemnest thyself; for thou *that* judgest doest the same things. Romans 2:1

This talks about pointing a finger at another. "You, you, you... You are no good. If it were not for you...you, you, you." "For wherein thou judgest another, thou condemnest thyself, for thou that judgest doeth the same things." When people are coming at you, accusing you in the victimization role that will allow the Unloving spirit of Rejection to come, they themselves have the same problem. You become the outlet for their frustration and Bitterness.

The hatred they have for themselves and the unloveliness they have concerning themselves is vented on you, so they do not have to deal with it themselves. You become the object of their own self-hatred and self-bitterness and unloveliness.

Because you are now on the receiving end and you are not spiritual, you then take that into yourself, and now you become an extension of it. That is the inherited curse in family trees, spiritually.

Iniquities are passed to the next generation when family members vent their stuff on you, and *you accept it* into yourself.

This will free you from what you inherited from your ancestry and give you back to God free of the Unloving spirit. Exodus says,

> Thou shalt not bow down thyself to them, nor serve them: for I the LORD thy God *am* a jealous God, visiting the iniquity of the fathers upon the children unto the third and fourth *generation* of them that hate me;
> Exodus 20:5

Ezekiel 18 seems to be a contradiction to Exodus 20, but it is not because this has to do with living and dying, or just not carrying the curse. Ezekiel says,

> [14]Now, lo, *if* he beget a son, that seeth all his father's sins which he hath done, and considereth, and doeth not such like,
> [15]That hath not eaten upon the mountains, neither hath lifted up his eyes to the idols of the house of Israel, hath not defiled his neighbour's wife,
> [16]Neither hath oppressed any, hath not withholden the pledge, neither hath spoiled by violence, *but* hath given his bread to the hungry, and hath covered the naked with a garment,
> [17]*That* hath taken off his hand from the poor, *that* hath not received usury nor increase, hath executed my judgments, hath walked in my statutes; he shall not die for the iniquity of his father, he shall surely live.
> [18]*As for* his father, because he cruelly oppressed, spoiled his brother by violence, and did *that* which *is* not good among his people, lo, even he shall die in his iniquity.
> Ezekiel 18:14-18

YOU CAN BE FREE

Now here is a promise that in spite of you inheriting the devastation of your ancestry, if you decide that you are going to walk in the statues of God, you can go free from the curse that is coming into you from your ancestry. Here is the promise of freedom. On the one hand we have the promise of the curse coming, but here is the promise of freedom. The son and the daughter do not have to die because of the sins of their fathers that have cursed them to death.

You do not have to die from the disease that your mother and father, grandmother and grandfather did. You can get right with God right now. You can receive His love, you can get it right with God and you can go free! You do not have to die of the diseases that are killing your ancestry because of their sins, even though it is passed on to you. Because you apply the principles, because you believe or apply the Word of God and walk in Him, you do not have to die because of your ancestral sins. You do not have to die; you can go free.

The Unloving spirit that was in your mother and your father or your grandmother or your grandfather or your great-grandmother or your great-grandfather that has been transferred from generation-to-generation breaking down the family tree in rage and anger, verbal abuse, physical abuse, emotional abuse, sexual abuse, drivenness and separation from love, you do not have to live with that any longer.

To be free,
you are going to have to receive
the love of God.

You have to make your peace with God. You need to be so willing to receive the love of God your Father in Jesus Christ that your perspective should be that if anyone smiles at you today, it is just a bonus. If you base your mental and spiritual welfare on the acceptance of another, then that is idolatry. You are making the person a god to yourself. When you do not receive the love of God, but you need the love of another first, that is idolatry. You are making that person a god to you and whether or not you are accepted, or you are loved depends on their acceptance of you.

But the Word says,

As it is written, There is none righteous, no, not one:
Romans 3:10

For all have sinned, and come short of the glory of God;
Romans 3:23

My chances of blowing it with you and you with me are very good. But the Bible says if we walk in the light as He is in the light, then we have fellowship one with another and when we blow it, the blood of Jesus cleanses both of us from the iniquity so we can get back into fellowship and walking in the light as He is in the light. That is the beginning of your freedom.

But if we walk in the light, as he is in the light, we have fellowship one with another, and the blood of Jesus Christ his Son cleanseth us from all sin.   1 John 1:7

You do not have to die for the sins of your father and mother. You must understand what came into you that broke you, injured you and caused the Unloving spirit, may have been in your generations and in your family tree for 5, 10, 15, 20, 30, 40 generations. This could be a family curse. When you look at your families and see the breakdown, you know it is true. *The same stuff you struggle with is what they struggled with, and what their daddy and mommy struggled with.* The breakdown of the family with each other is complete. The Unloving spirit is responsible.

An Unloving spirit in you will keep you from receiving the love of God, it will keep you from loving yourself, and it will keep you from loving others and receiving the love of others.

First John says,

There is no fear in love; but perfect love casteth out fear: because fear hath torment. He that feareth is not made perfect in love. 1 John 4:18

The absence of love in part one of this scripture brings Fear. It means you do not have the ability to give and receive love without Fear and that is proof of the presence of the Unloving spirit. Fear of man, Fear of rejection, Fear of failure and Fear of abandonment are fertile ground for the Unloving spirit to rule you.

This is between you and God, but you need to prepare your heart spiritually. The Bible says you need to honor your mother and your father, and that is often misquoted, which allows abuse. You are to honor God over mother and father. In fact, the Bible says that if you will leave mother and father and husbands and wives, and brothers and sisters, and houses and lands for the cause of the gospel, God shall give to you in this lifetime an hundredfold, mothers and fathers, brothers and sisters, houses, and lands; and in the world to come, eternal life.

Here you see you can leave mother and father for the cause of God for your own safety and it is permissible. *You have to get on here and decide which family you are going to be part of, the dead family influenced by evil spirits or the family of the living God. This is your choice.* Now at the same time, you do not abandon your family in your prayers because the Bible says you cannot abandon your family. It says you must be diligent towards your family even when they are in sin. So you pray for them and ask God to deal with them, and then you live your life before God in purity.

You can be free and the issues between your mother and your father and your family do not have to be resolved, but they must be resolved between you and God. If you are waiting for those issues to be resolved before you can be healed and be whole, you are wasting your time, because again, you have made unspiritual people responsible for your spirituality. What you are saying is, "If they will get right spiritually, I will." No, you get right spiritually in spite of them.

INIQUITIES OF YOUR FAMILY TREE

List everything in your life that is contributing to your Rejection, your self-rejection, your self-hatred and the Unloving spirit that came to you from someone else. List the people and their names, whether they are alive or whether they are dead. That can include mother, father, brother, sister, dog, the boss, your pastor, anyone that has violated you in the area of trust and love that has allowed the unclean, Unloving spirit to become part of your life. This is so you can recognize those dynamics in your family tree that are not of God, and for you to identify those areas that are in your own personal life that you now have, that should not be there.

To defeat this, x-ray your enemy as clearly as you can. Look at every speck of his existence and cause this whole thing to come into transparency and into a place of identification. Take those parts of you that you do not want to deal with, and bring them struggling to the table and lay them before God.

It has to be faced. It is time for you to move on. Why should you die because of the sins of your fathers? Ezekiel 18 says you do not have to. You may have inherited their sins, but you do not have to die in them. That is what Jesus made possible for you. He bore the penalty of the curse in His body.

Prepare to lay down self-rejection. Prepare to leave mother and father for the cause of the gospel. When it says to honor your mother and father, it means only to the degree that they honor God in their own personal lives. When they do not, you are not bound to honor them in their sin.

Do not honor people in their sin.

The Bible is also very clear about spouses. It says if the unbelieving elect to live at home in peace with a believing wife, she is to allow him to remain because he might be won to Christ by her chaste conversation.

> [12]But to the rest speak I, not the Lord: If any brother hath a wife that believeth not, and she be pleased to dwell with him, let him not put her away.
>
> [13]And the woman which hath an husband that believeth not, and if he be pleased to dwell with her, let her not leave him.
>
> [14]For the unbelieving husband is sanctified by the wife, and the unbelieving wife is sanctified by the husband: else were your children unclean; but now are they holy.
>
> [15]But if the unbelieving depart, let him depart. A brother or a sister is not under bondage in such *cases:* but God hath called us to peace.
>
> [16]For what knowest thou, O wife, whether thou shalt save *thy* husband? or how knowest thou, O man, whether thou shalt save *thy* wife?   1 Corinthians 7:12-16

> [1]Likewise, ye wives, *be* in subjection to your own husbands; that, if any obey not the word, they also may without the word be won by the conversation of the wives;
>
> [2]While they behold your chaste conversation *coupled* with fear.   1 Peter 3:1-2

LIVE TOGETHER IN PEACE

The key is being able to live together in peace. If there is an unsaved husband and the wife is saved, and he is a roaring maniac in the home, into physical, emotional, verbal and

43

sexual abuse, it is time for separation because the Bible says, "If at all possible, live peaceably one with another."

If it be possible, as much as lieth in you, live peaceably with all men. Romans 12:18

Where there is strife, there is every evil thing.

For where envying and strife *is*, there *is* confusion and every evil work. James 3:16

Do not condone evil. The Bible says,

For where your treasure is, there will your heart be also. Matthew 6:21

To make sure this marriage is of God and they love each other, get them to separate for awhile. Then see where the love is. In relationships, you get it together or get out of it because anything less than that is evil. But there is a place of prayer and a place of longsuffering and a place of time and space that must be built into it to the degree there is no abuse or victimization.

We have to come to a place where we can live peaceably one with another. The Bible is very clear, if the unbelieving member of that marriage elects to stay with the believer and live in peace, then that unbelieving member is allowed to stay because there is always a chance for conversion. But that is conditional on living in peace.

The things that were in that person who wounded you in marriage were also in his parents. In every generation it was there. It happened to your mommy and daddy, your grandmommy and granddaddy, and it has been there for generations. We have had many generations of devastation from Adam.

44

You have inherited an Unloving spirit from your ancestry, and you are dressed up in it yourself every single day to some degree. You must realize what being born again is all about. You must understand what is meant by the scriptures that say you are a new creation. You are a new creature by faith. You are not a biological seed of your ancestry anymore. If you keep hanging onto your biological ancestry, you negate the sonship and daughtership of the living God.

"Well, I don't want to let my family go."

No, I do not want to let my family go either, but I certainly want to let go of what is in my family that is not of God. The Bible is very clear, we are all part of our families, but you have to get a more accurate picture of who you are. You are now being restored to your real Father, and your real Father is God the Father. When you die and the angels transport your spirit and your soul into the third heaven, your biological family no longer exists, on any dimension. You will see them in heaven and you will remember the days that you possibly had, because the Bible says you will be known as you are known.

> **For now we see through a glass, darkly; but then face to face: now I know in part; but then shall I know even as also I am known.** 1 Corinthians 13:12

But you are going to change the dimension when you go on into eternity, and it will not be a biological family; it will be a heavenly family. Start preparing to separate yourself from your biological families and the evil spirits working in them. It may already be stirring everything that can be stirred up. You are just boiling behind the scenes. Inside, you are already in torment.

We will put the finger of God on you until you either submit to God, or you become an enemy forever. Not many

45

churches will deal with things at this level, because most of the time when this stuff surfaces in people and they can't separate themselves from it, they attack the leadership. If the devil can eliminate me from you, he is safe in you. If the devil can eliminate me and my forward motion as a warrior against your enemy, he can effectively continue to inhabit your land.

So you are going to have to get it very clear whether I am a friend or an enemy. If you make me the enemy, you are deceived. That thing inside of you that is binding you and putting you in bondage is your enemy. God is not your enemy. Jesus is not your enemy. The Holy Spirit is not your enemy. The leadership that is set over you is not your enemy. The devil is your enemy.

DO YOU REALLY WANT TO BE FREE?

You may have a struggle in determining whether or not you want to be free. Many people love feeling rejected. They love feeling unloved. They love being angry. They love being sassy. They love slander. They love gossip. They love Bitterness. They love Rejection. They love Fear. It is a way of life. You say, "It is just the way I am; if you do not like it, too bad." *Where did that come from? I set myself apart before God to defeat the enemy of mankind. If you want to be free, then take your freedom.*

The easiest thing in the world would be to placate you: to pat you on the back, say sweet nothing prayers over you and never challenge you in who you are and what you are dealing with. That is basically where the church is today. It does not really challenge anyone too much because it is afraid of hurting someone's feelings. People might get mad at them. The leadership, for the most part, has been attacked over the years. They are so paranoid. Their families, their

46

wives and their children are so attacked by the sheep they're trying to help that they do not even try anymore. They show up, they preach a little sermon, they put little Band-Aids on, and the pastor goes home. The people go home just as sick as they were when they walked in. No one wants to confront issues anymore because of Fear of man, Fear of rejection and Fear of failure.

Did you ever see anyone dressed up in rage and anger? Did you ever see anyone dressed up in self-hatred? Did you ever see anyone dressed up in lust? Did you ever see anyone dressed up in Self-Pity, or with an Unloving spirit, or Envy and Jealousy, or in Rejection? It does not take much discernment. They are dressed up in it – like putting on a jacket. Your devil knows you better than you know yourself. It is time to take authority over your life. Luke says,

> 9And I say unto you, Ask, and it shall be given you; seek, and ye shall find; knock, and it shall be opened unto you.
> 10For every one that asketh receiveth; and he that seeketh findeth; and to him that knocketh it shall be opened.
> 11If a son shall ask bread of any of you that is a father, will he give him a stone? or if *he ask* a fish, will he for a fish give him a serpent?
> 12Or if he shall ask an egg, will he offer him a scorpion?
> 13If ye then, being evil, know how to give good gifts unto your children: how much more shall *your* heavenly Father give the Holy Spirit to them that ask him?   Luke 11:9-13

This has to do with answered prayer. What are you asking for? What are you looking for? What are you knocking about? If a son shall ask bread of any of you that is a father will he give him a stone? Or if he asks a fish, will he for a fish give him a serpent? Or if he shall ask for an egg, will he offer him a scorpion? If you then being evil know how to give good gifts unto your children, how much more shall your heavenly Father give the Holy Spirit to them that ask Him? This is a wonderful scripture about receiving the Baptism of the Holy Spirit.

Epilepsy

And he was casting out a devil, and it was dumb. And it came to pass, when the devil was gone out, the dumb spake; and the people wondered.   Luke 11:14

Jesus was casting out a devil, and it was dumb. That person could not speak. There is an evil spirit behind that, and that spirit controls the muscular processes, the mind and everything so that the person is unable to speak. There is nothing wrong with the person; they just have a dumb devil.

Sometimes there are certain genetic things that can happen or there are certain injuries that can happen, but most of the people who are dumb have a spirit behind it. Epilepsy is an evil spirit that needs to be cast out. In epilepsy the evil spirit interferes with the brain waves, producing an aberration which causes an epileptic seizure.

"Jesus was casting out a devil, and it was dumb. It came to pass that when the devil was gone out, the dumb spake." What was the nature of that evil spirit? Its full function as an evil spirit was to keep that person from speaking.

Every evil spirit you have within you has a function. It will keep you from receiving love, or it will keep you from giving love. If you are unable to give and receive love, if you are unable to receive love because you have an Unloving, unclean spirit, you can either decide you want to keep that spiritual parasite that is keeping you from being who God created you to be, or you can make up your mind you have had enough and get rid of it.

It's amazing how you blow your nose to clean it out, but you won't blow your spirit to clean it out. It's amazing how
48

you will take authority over everyone else in your life, but you won't take authority over the things that are destructive to your life. You spend so much time blaming everyone else around you, why don't you blame the devil?

It is time for the devil to get a spiritual headache and for you to recognize your enemy. When I say "devil," I'm not talking about him personally; I'm talking about the kingdom that answers to him, ruling mankind. It's time for him to be tormented, not you.

"Jesus was casting out a devil and it was dumb. It came to pass when the devil was gone out, the dumb spake and the people wondered." This individual now could speak, and before he could not speak. The devil had to go before he could speak. In the same way, the Unloving spirit is going to have to go out of you before you can learn to love yourself. Instead of being a dumb spirit that keeps you from speaking, it is an Unloving spirit that keeps you from receiving love. There is no difference here, just a different application.

Do you think God created you to *not* be able to "receive" love? Do you think God created you to *not* be able to "give" love? Do you think God created you to *not* be able to "enjoy" love? If you do, then you violate the Scriptures because they say, "God is love." God is not having a problem today loving Himself. He thinks He is pretty hot stuff. Why? Because He is and He accepts it. Do you think God has any problem with His identity? Do you think Jesus has any problem with His identity? Do you think the Holy Ghost has any problem with His identity? Do you think angels have any problem with their identity?

Do you think devils have any problem with their identity? No, they love it. They love being devils. An evil spirit loves being what it is. That's its nature. It loves being murderous. It loves slander. It loves people who hurt others.

49

It wants you to have a miserable day because in the day you have a miserable day; it is having a good day. There is a scripture that says, "When an evil spirit is cast out it wanders through a dry place looking for a place of rest."

> When the unclean spirit is gone out of a man, he walketh through dry places, seeking rest; and finding none, he saith, I will return unto my house whence I came out. Luke 11:24

When it was in the person it was at rest. Now that it is out, it is in torment because it has no medium of expression, and it is stuck with every foul desire of its nature and no way to express itself, so it needs you. The Unloving spirit needs you. Bitterness needs you. Envy and Jealousy need you. Rage and anger need you. Rejection needs you. Lust needs you. Because without you they do not have any way to express themselves, and are in torment until they do.

If there is an evil spirit within you, it will manifest in your lifetime by its nature. It will strategize through you, it will set up scenarios through you until you finally yield to its nature, its thoughts, its presence, its emotions, and it will manifest. I know people who are murderous and have murder in their heart against their brother, and I stand a chance of getting lynched like everyone else does. The spirit that I see in them will manifest at some point because that spirit is in its place of rest and peace.

It is time the church started teaching about the second heaven.

The church is so busy teaching about everything, they have forgotten to teach their people the knowledge of evil, instead of just the knowledge of good. Hebrews 5:14 says you are able to handle strong meat. You are a person by reason of exercise of your senses, able to discern both good and evil, not just good. I want someone to tell me when something is evil.

I tell my kids what is not good for them. I told my kids the other day, "If you do not get a grip on this, this disease will come upon you in your generation."

You say, "You cursed them."

No I did not curse them. I gave them the Word of God. I do not put any pressure on my children.

I tell them, "You do the best you can in school. Be who God created you to be. I do not even know what that is. All I can do is teach you the way you should go."

The environment helps set the stage for God to come, but there are people in good environments that are having spiritual problems. The environment does not necessarily shape the child. It can affect the child, but maybe the child needs to be delivered of things inherited from his ancestry.

Boils

We worked with a child one time who was very rebellious and very angry, and he would be honest about it. He had boils; sometimes he would have four to eight boils at a time, and they were very bad boils all over his body. It was inherited. His father had boils, and he had boils. Deuteronomy 28:27 says boils are a curse that comes out of disobedience. We told him, "So here is the deal, if you want your boils, stay in rebellion. If you do not want your boils then submit to God and get this rebellious spirit out of you."

He came before God, and he repented. Sincerely, he cried out to God. We told him, "The exchange for your boils is your obedience." We ministered to him, went before God, and he repented for that spirit of rebellion in him that he inherited. He was in agreement, and we cast rebellion out of him. Within two days the boils were gone.

About nine months later, all of a sudden the child slipped into some stuff, and *within 24 hours* after he made a very bad spiritual decision in a rebellious area, a boil had popped right up on him, just like that. He came looking for help. He said, "I'm in trouble. I slipped back into rebellion and here (the boil) is the fruit of it. I am ready to deal with it."

We went before God, he repented and overnight the boil disappeared. He has never had one since. If you would ask him about rebellion and boils, he will tell you that with sin comes a consequence.

IT MUST BE CAST OUT

Did you know there are a lot of people who want stuff cast out of them, but they are not really in agreement? They want to be free of the boil, but they do not want to change in their rebellion. If you want God to fix you, but you do not want to change the spiritual dynamics in your life producing the problem, we are all wasting our time. You must submit to the living God. If you want to be free of diseases that have a spiritual root, you are going to have to deal with the spiritual root.

Are you really willing to remove the spiritual root that is producing the problem?

Reading this may be irritating you. The feeling of irritation you may be noticing is that spirit in you: it hates the truth. I am putting my finger right on it, and it does not want to operate in light. It wants to operate in darkness. It needs you; it wants you. It does not want to give you up. All these little feelings you have on the inside are not even you to begin with. That spirit is strategizing to hang onto you, like a roach looking for a place to hide. Here comes the spotlight of God on your life, and it goes running here or there. So you are trying to avoid that light because of the Unloving spirit.

Jesus was casting out a dumb spirit and when the dumb spirit was gone, the individual could speak. But some people said, "He casteth out devils through Beelzebub the chief of the devils."

> 14And he was casting out a devil, and it was dumb. And it came to pass, when the devil was gone out, the dumb spake; and the people wondered.
> 15But some of them said, He casteth out devils through Beelzebub the chief of the devils.   Luke 11:14-15

They were saying that Jesus was of the devil, and that He was casting out devils by the power of the devil.

There are churches that believe a Christian cannot have a devil. I was ministering to a person who had a disease that was caused by a devil, and I spoke, "In the name of Jesus, spirit of Fear, come out."

A woman jumped up in my face and said, "You can't do that. That person's a Christian. He does not have a devil of Fear."

I said, "The evidence is right here."

She looked at me and said, "You are of the devil."

I looked her back right square in the eye and said, "I command you in the name of Jesus to reply to me." I said, "If I cast an evil spirit out in the name of the Lord Jesus Christ, am I casting that spirit out by the power of the Holy Spirit or by the power of the devil? I command you to answer me."

She would not answer me.

I said, "You have accused the Holy Spirit of being the devil. If I, in the name of Jesus, cast out an evil spirit in the

53

name of Jesus, by whose spirit do I cast it out? The Holy Spirit or the devil? I command an answer."

She refused to answer. I said, "You haven't answered me because if you said "of the devil," you are damned forever and that is blasphemy against the Holy Spirit."

Blasphemy against the Holy Spirit is attributing the works of the Holy Spirit to the devil. Do you know how many people in churches are going to hell today for that reason? *Blasphemy against the Holy Spirit is calling the Holy Spirit "Satan" and saying that what you are doing is by the power of the devil instead of by the power of the Holy Spirit.* It is a very serious offense.

That thing within you is not even you. Do you think you were born with an Unloving spirit? Probably. But do you think that is what God created you with? Do you think when God said in Genesis, "Let us create man in our own image," and He created Adam and Eve and said it was very good, that He created them to be all goofed up spiritually? Do you think He said, "This is wonderful. This is my goofed up child in whom I am well pleased. I love my son and my daughter although they do not love themselves."

There are things like Rejection and Bitterness and the Unloving spirit, and the stuff that they call emotional problems. Do you know why this stuff bugs you so bad, and why you don't like it? It is because it's foreign to you. God did not create you to enjoy it or to have fellowship with it or for it to be part of you. If you were created to have pain and problems on the inside, if you were created to have depression and an Unloving spirit and self-rejection and self-hatred, if you were created for that reason, then it would be normal to you.

54

You would say, "I am depressed today. Boy, it is about time. I can't stand this mental peace. It is foreign to me. I need someone to hate today. I need to find someone to get into trouble with. I can't stand loving myself. Every time I look at that guy, he is smiling. That hypocrite! I can't stand that smile. I want to have a wonderful day of hatred. I do not feel good, and that is just the way it is supposed to be. Do not ask me to smile; no one can make me smile. You say you love me? Huh! Prove it! It is just the way I am. No one will love me anyway." The more you try to prove it, the more they reject you. That is not you. That is a dumb devil that has become part of your life.

Luke says,

> ¹⁶And others, tempting *him,* sought of him a sign from heaven.
> ¹⁷But he, knowing their thoughts, said unto them, Every kingdom divided against itself is brought to desolation; and a house *divided* against a house falleth.
> ¹⁸If Satan also be divided against himself, how shall his kingdom stand? because ye say that I cast out devils through Beelzebub.
> ¹⁹And if I by Beelzebub cast out devils, by whom do your sons cast *them* out? therefore shall they be your judges.
> Luke 11:16-19

Do you know what Jesus is saying? "If I am having success casting out devils by the power of the devil, then who is delivering you? But if I by Beelzebub cast out devils, by whom do your sons cast them out? Therefore they shall be your judges." What is Jesus saying? There is no one dealing with your spiritual problems to begin with. You are just all goofed up and running around with disease and insanity, and here is this man who is now able to speak. Which one of you was able to cast out that dumb devil and give him the ability to speak again? Which one of your sons is doing it?

Look at verse 20.

> But if I with the finger of God cast out devils, no doubt
> the kingdom of God is come upon you.   Luke 11:20

If you are able to remove the Unloving spirit, what has come upon you? The kingdom of God! If the Unloving spirit still remains with you, what has come upon you? The kingdom of the devil! Now do you want to hang onto the kingdom of the devil, or do you want to get the kingdom of God in your life? But if I with the finger of God cast out devils, no doubt the kingdom of God has come upon you.

Can I challenge you in your thinking? When you call yourself a man or woman of God, and you say, "Yes Lord, I love You. Thanks for saving me. I am a son (or daughter) of God. I am saved. I am redeemed. I am here to establish the kingdom of God." Then what about those ten spiritual areas of your life that you refuse to deal with? Are you establishing the kingdom of God in those areas? Everything you do not deal with in your life spiritually that is from the devil, is dividing the kingdom of God in your life. Do you want the kingdom of God to come upon you in fullness?

You say, "I want to be filled with the Holy Ghost." He is God. He comes in to lead you into all truth. But maybe you do not want to know about this or that, and the first thing you know, you put the Holy Ghost back in the back bedroom of your house. Then you go to that back bedroom only when you need Him, but when He comes out to convict you and deal with you concerning the other parts of the kingdom of Satan that are in your life, you tell the Holy Ghost, "Leave me alone, this is my house." The Holy Ghost withdraws. The worst thing I can do is try to set someone free who does not want to be set free. I am wasting my time.

If I with the finger of God cast out devils, no doubt the kingdom of God has come upon you. When a strong man armed keepeth his palace, his goods are in peace. But when one stronger than he shall come upon him and overcome him, he taketh from him all his armor wherein he trusted and divideth his spoils. He that is not with me is against me, and he that gathereth not with me scattereth.

> ²¹When a strong man armed keepeth his palace, his goods are in peace:
> ²²But when a stronger than he shall come upon him, and overcome him, he taketh from him all his armour wherein he trusted, and divideth his spoils.
> ²³He that is not with me is against me: and he that gathereth not with me scattereth...   Luke 11:21-23

When a strong man armed keepeth his palace, his goods are in peace. *You* are the palace. Your sovereign house you live in is the palace. Do you know you live in a palace? You look in the palace and say, "Hello palace, how are you doing? I love living in you. You are the temple of God. You are the palace of the living God. You are the temple of the most high God." You are supposed to be enjoying your house. When that disease comes, does it keep you from enjoying your house that you are living in? When the winds of confusion come into your mind with depression and Rejection, and the Unloving spirits, do they affect your living quarters? It is like leaving the windows open in the middle of a blizzard, and you wonder why you have snow in the house.

RULE YOUR OWN SPIRIT

The Bible says that the man who has no rule over his own spirit is like a city with its walls broken down, and all the beasts of the field run in.

> He that *hath* no rule over his own spirit *is like* a city *that is* broken down, *and* without walls.　　　Proverbs 25:28

> For thou shalt be in league with the stones of the field: and the beasts of the field shall be at peace with thee.
> 　　　Job 5:23

You are just saying, "Come on in," and then you wonder why you have spiritual problems in your life. "Oh, Rejection. Hello, come on in. You have to say what about what? Oh self-hatred come on in; you have what to say about me? You are right. That is exactly who I am. I am a worm. I am no one. No one loves me. I am the worst of the worst."

The Word says that of those born of women, there is none greater than John the Baptist.

> Verily I say unto you, Among them that are born of women there hath not risen a greater than John the Baptist: notwithstanding he that is least in the kingdom of *heaven* is greater than he.　　　Matthew 11:11

The Bible does not say it was Mary, but that it was John the Baptist. But he that is least in the kingdom of God is greater than John the Baptist. When you say you are no one and you call yourself saved, you are not in the kingdom of God. You are in the kingdom of the devil, because if you are the least of us all you are greater than John the Baptist.

If you are condemning yourself by words of the Unloving spirit, remember that the words of your mouth are life or death. The meditations of your heart are life or death. If you are repeating unloving words that others have told you, that is the curse that came to reinforce itself. Now your house is divided. A house divided against itself cannot stand.

> And Jesus knew their thoughts, and said unto them, Every kingdom divided against itself is brought to desolation; and every city or house divided against itself shall not stand:
> 　　　Matthew 12:25

A house divided against itself cannot stand. A double minded man is unstable in all his ways.

> **A double minded man *is* unstable in all his ways.**
>
> James 1:8

If you are not careful with this Unloving spirit, this self-rejection and self-hatred, you have one foot in the kingdom of God that says God loves you, and the other foot in the kingdom of Satan that says you are not loved. You are torn and buffeted. The Bible says why do you halt between two opinions?

> **And Elijah came unto all the people, and said, How long halt ye between two opinions? if the LORD *be* God, follow him: but if Baal, *then* follow him. And the people answered him not a word.** 1 Kings 18:21

Why do you halt between two opinions? You are to hold every thought in captivity; every thought, every imagination must be held up against the knowledge of God, casting down everything that is not what God said.

> **Casting down imaginations, and every high thing that exalteth itself against the knowledge of God, and bringing into captivity every thought to the obedience of Christ;**
>
> 2 Corinthians 10:5

When you have one foot here and one foot there, you are halting between two opinions. A double minded man is unstable in all his ways. You can't serve two masters. You will either love one or hate the other.

> **A double minded man *is* unstable in all his ways.**
>
> James 1:8

> **No man can serve two masters: for either he will hate the one, and love the other; or else he will hold to the one, and despise the other. Ye cannot serve God and mammon.**
>
> Matthew 6:24

Are you serving God or the devil? When you do not love yourself, you are calling God a liar, and you are telling Him He made a mistake when He created you.

In ministry when I have a spirit that will not obey me when I want to cast it out of someone, I say, "Hey you, I told you to leave in the name of Jesus."

"I am not going. You can't make me. I'm staying right here."

"Listen, you are a spirit. You have access to heaven. Do you see the Father right there on the throne? Hi Papa, how are You doing? This little foul spirit will not obey me. Now you spirit, you go right up to the throne and tell Father God that you do not have to obey me."

"Well, you know I can't do that."

When you are in that place of believing God, that He has accepted you and loved you, when that Unloving spirit that is tormenting you in your mind comes up, you tell it, "You, get up there to the Father, and you tell Him that He does not love me. You tell Him that He is a liar. I am not going to make God a liar."

If you will get that serious about your life, God will meet you, and if you do not, He will not. If you want to hate yourself, God is not going to stop you.

"Well, God can just come down here."

No, you are down here. You take authority over the affairs of the earth. God put you here to be a king and a priest in the making. God put you here to have dominion. You take dominion over that invisible world. You take authority over your life. You decide you are going to be a man or woman of God. You decide what you are going to do, and you choose this day what you shall have, blessings or cursings, life or death. If you chose death and cursings, then it will come onto you. Then you surface the next day and say, "I need prayer. It is not going well. I am struggling."

What decisions did you make in your heart yesterday?

"Well, I do not like feeling unloved."

Then why did you allow it to become part of your thinking yesterday?

"Well..."

I want to tell you something: I have accepted the love of God, just the way I am. You know I am unperfected, and you know I have a ways to go. Let those secret thoughts out... You know I blow it. You know I am not perfect. You know it, because you verbalize it. But do you know what? I am loved of God in spite of you! Praise the Lord! If it were not for that, I would be teaching you from inside this pulpit thinking, God give me the grace to face these fiery darts. "I'm the pastor. I have come to you in the name of Jesus to teach you the Word of God and I really love God." God, can I really stand here and speak for You? I say, "Good morning sheep. Any goats out there?" God, there are fiery darts.

I love you guys, no matter what the devil says to you about me. I understand the war and the warfare. You need to understand the warfare, and you need to understand the war. God has given you all the tools you need to defeat the powers of darkness. You do not have to remind me of my weaknesses, because I have a devil that is assigned to me too. I get a revelation in the spirit before I ever see it in your faces. All you're doing is confirming it. It is too real, isn't it? But I am loved of God. I am not plagued in my identity.

It does not mean that I am not attacked in my identity, because we all are. You are not immune to temptation; you are not immune to fiery darts. You are not immune to the attacks of the devil even in the areas that you have been delivered from. The devil is a sore loser. Jesus defeated Satan in His day of temptation, and the Word says that Satan left him for a season.

Satan went back at some point, chewing in His ears. "You are who? You are the son of God? Prove it. Well, haven't you read in Isaiah that you are going to be killed? I am going to get you, Jesus."

Jesus said, "Haven't you read that the temple that is cast down. On the third day God shall raise it up?"

First Corinthians 2:8 says if the devil had known that by crucifying the Lord of Glory he would have been defeated, he would have never allowed it to happen. But he was so bent on destruction, so driven by his own deceptions and his misguided Bitterness, that he forgot to read the Bible all the way.

The house (the body) that you live in belongs to God, and it is on loan to you, so quit criticizing yourself. For that matter, if your ancestral line has been through hell and you are comparing yourself to other houses that people live in, you miss the whole thing because in the resurrection you are going to get a new house, an eternal house. Why lose your life and forfeit your future? Your house belongs to you, and your spirit is your own. That is really who you are supposed to be. Your soul is your own, and your body is your own. It's your sovereignty. But in many of your lives an invader has come, who is sitting in your chair eating your lunch, sleeping in your bed, running your life for you, while you are spiritually downstairs in a basement prison house. He is armed and he is a strong man and he is taking you over. Luke says,

> When a strong man armed keepeth his palace, his goods
> are in peace: Luke 11:21

What are his goods? The Unloving spirit is a principality, and he is trusting that Bitterness will keep him entrenched in your house. He is trusting that resentment and retaliation, and anger and hatred, and violence and murder, and unforgiveness will keep him entrenched in your house.

He is banking on the fact that Envy and Jealousy will keep him in control of your house. He is banking on the fact that Rejection will keep him in control of your house. He is banking on the fact that the Unloving spirit within you will keep him entrenched in your house. He is banking on the fact that guilt and self-rejection, and self-hatred and lack of self-esteem are going to keep him in your house. He is banking on all the underling spirits that reinforce his position and rulership in your life, to keep him in your house. If you're listening to them, Jesus is not your lord, the devil is.

In everyday life we make Satan our lord, but not in all areas. Is Jesus Christ Lord of your life in all areas yet? You know He isn't. But in your heart do you want Him to be? God is not judging you after the possession of Satan in your life, but He is judging you after His intent and His love and His will for your life in the future. He is helping you as a work of the Holy Spirit to work out your salvation daily. So if we put the finger of God on your heart and show you the dark creatures that are running around stealing your life and stealing from you, do not get mad at God, do not get mad at me, do not get mad at yourself. Instead say, "Thank God for discernment, and the power of God to be delivered."

Without discernment, without teaching and without God you are stuck with this evil until you die.

Now do you want to be stuck with evil until you die? Or do you want to be free? Your house belongs to you. Say, "My house belongs to me." Do you really mean that? Then why are you allowing the space invaders to stay with you? If there was a frog in some of your houses, you would call the fire department out here, and you would be on top of the roof. You would ask for help to get rid of it. It is amazing how we don't deal with some things in our lives.

Do you want to love yourself? Do you want to accept yourself? Do you want to feel good about yourself? Are you able to feel good about yourself and still have unrenewed things in your life? Are you able to accept and love yourself even though you have not finished the reconstruction of your house?

If you were remodeling your home right now, would you hate your home because it was not fully remodeled? No you wouldn't. You have the vision of what the house is going to look like when you have finished the remodeling. You have the drawing, you have the picture, and you know what it is going to look like. You know what is going to be on the walls, you know the color, and you know what the finished product is going to look like.

In the midst of the dust, and the mess, and the noise, and the chaos, your heart is rejoicing because the thing is under reconstruction, and you are joyful in your mess. You are accepting the mess in your home and yourself in the mess, because you know the object of your faith and your hope, and your house is under construction. The worst thing that can happen to you is to be in that dilapidated old house and there be no hope for reconstruction. Then you get into despair and hopelessness, because you are stuck in your deal.

But, you are not stuck in your deal. When Jesus cast out that dumb spirit, that man was not stuck in his deal any longer. One day he could not speak, and the next day he could speak. One day you may hate yourself and the next day after Jesus comes and delivers you, you may love yourself. Wouldn't that be a wonderful exchange? Do you want to speak, or do you just want to be dumb? If you were dumb and couldn't speak right now, if you had a choice, would you like to talk? If Jesus came along and cast the dumb spirit out so that you could talk, wouldn't you rejoice?

Then you ought to have the same mentality about everything in your life that needs to go. You should be excited about the fact that you are going to be able to love yourself, and you are going to be able to have your peace. You can start loving yourself today while all the details of your life are not worked out, because you have faith and you have joy and you have hope and you know what God is doing in your life.

I am at peace with myself, and I am totally unperfected. I know where I have come from. This is a powerful axiom of truth. Say it with me:

**I am not what I was, and I am not what I shall be.
I am in a state of change from glory to glory.**

God loved you in your unperfectedness just as much as He is going to love you in your perfectedness. His love for you is not based on you being totally fixed. He loved you from the beginning, and He does not love you any more when you have it all together. In fact, the Word says in your weakness He is made strong. His heart as a Father is to fix you.

But what if you do not want to be fixed? Do you remember the child with the boils? What if he did not want to get out of rebellion? Did he want to be free of his boils? What was the condition of being free from his boils? Get out of rebellion. It is a fair exchange, isn't it? Start making a list of everything surrounding this unloveliness that has to go.

You will see it in your family tree. You will see it in your mommy, daddy, grandmommy, granddaddy, great-grandmommy, and great-granddaddy. You will see it in yourself. If you have children, you are seeing some of it already showing up in your own children. If it is not dealt with it will show up in their children because that is what has been happening to mankind. Now where do you think it should stop? Right here. With you.

YOUR HOUSE IS YOUR TEMPLE

Now, this is the house you live in, but it says here in Luke that someone has taken you over. A strong man armed keepeth his palace; his goods are in peace. The Bible says, "Except you bind the strong man, you cannot spoil his house." You cannot take away his dastardly deeds. Is Rejection a dastardly deed? What about an Unloving spirit, is that dastardly deed good? It is not part of you.

I can see you now building a house out here and you say, "You know what? The floor is too clean. I need to go down to the creek and bring in some mud." So you get a bucket full of mud and say, "I can't stand this clean floor. I am an unclean person, and I am going to live in my clean house with a dirty floor." Then you smear the whole floor with mud because you do not want your floor to be clean. In spiritual application, there are some people who want to look good on the outside, but they do not want to clean the inside. Many houses look good on the outside, but the inside is not too good. They do not keep up with it very well.

"When one stronger than he shall come upon him and overcome him, he taketh from him all his armor wherein he trusted and divideth his spoils."

But when a stronger than he shall come upon him, and overcome him, he taketh from him all his armour wherein he trusted, and divideth his spoils. Luke 11:22

In ministry, we want to take away the armor that strong man is trusting in. You are like a collage: you have bits and pieces pasted to you of different pictures of life and it is not really the full picture. Collages do not give you a distinct picture of anything; they just give you a mixture of this and that. What your life has become is a collage of things that do not belong in the picture. They are disjointed and dissimilar; they are not part of the picture. That is the armor that your strong man is trusting in.

Your house belongs to you and was given to you from God. Your enemy, the strong man that controls your palace, is deciding that what he has put into you from your ancestry and from your personal life is not going to be touched or bothered. He figures you belong to him, your house belongs to him, and he is safe and secure in it while you are down peeping out from the bars of your prison house. He is content that he can rule you the rest of your days.

Are you satisfied with that? Do you want to strip off the Bitterness, the Envy and Jealousy, the divination, the Unloving spirit, the Rejection, the insecurities? Do you want to strip this stuff off and remove this armor to make that strong man vulnerable? The strong man is weak. His strength comes from the pawns that he has put in your life. He is trusting in his armor. He is trusting in the way you think, that he has become so much a part of you that he can

67

control you, and he can rule you forever. Are you in agreement with that?

You need to identify the aspects of your thoughts that will keep you from loving yourself and identify those same aspects in your family tree. Get rid of those thoughts that are accusing you to yourself.

Editor's Note: For more information, *Accusing Spirits* is available from the **Be in Health**™ Bookstore.

The Bible says the accuser of the brethren, who accused them before their God day and night, is cast down.

> And I heard a loud voice saying in heaven, Now is come salvation, and strength, and the kingdom of our God, and the power of his Christ: for the accuser of our brethren is cast down, which accused them before our God day and night.
>
> Revelation 12:10

SEPARATION LEADS TO DISEASE

An Unloving spirit is something that makes you feel unlovely. It makes you feel guilty. It makes you feel unclean, makes you feel like you are a "nobody." It makes you feel like no one loves you. It makes you feel like you are the last thing in the world that should have been created by God. It projects out through your eyes and knows that everyone knows you just aren't worth it. It will not give you the ability to be at peace with yourself, day and night, night and day.

IT BEGAN IN THE GARDEN

The beginning of all disease that has a spiritual root is separation from God, separation from yourself and separation from others. The beginning of all healing begins in restoration of your relationship with God according to how the Scriptures say it should be. It begins right in Genesis. One of the first areas of separation from a

68

relationship with God comes out of sin. It was God's custom to walk in the cool of the evening with Adam and Eve in the garden. That word God is *Elohiym*, which is Jesus Christ in His preincarnate state, the very individual who created them by His spoken word. It is that same individual who came and died for you and is coming again to bring you to Himself. He is the bridegroom, and you are the virgin, spiritually. That is the bottom line.

You are the spiritual virgin. He is the bridegroom; He is your eternal husband of the future, whether you are male or female. You are going to have to get the antichrist spirit out of your being if you are going to ever be free of an Unloving spirit. You are going to have to accept God the Father, God the Word and God the Holy Spirit once and for all, unconditionally.

Otherwise Satan will be your father and every foul, unclean spirit that answers to him will inhabit your space. They are designed to separate you from God's love; they are designed to separate you from yourself and to separate you from others. You are going to have to get this one down and get it engraved on the tables of your heart once and for all. To the degree you do not, is the degree your life will be devastated in your relationship with God, your relationship with yourself and your relationship with others.

It is amazing you won't let certain people do certain things to you, but you will let invisible beings do it to you.

FAITH IS ESSENTIAL

The Bible says very clearly in Hebrews 4 that those who came out of Egypt are just like you. They did not enter into promise because they didn't obey the Word. The same Word preached to them is the same Word being preached to you. They entered not into their place of rest, and they did not enter into their place of promise because they did not mix the Word they heard with faith. They did not believe it.

>¹Let us therefore fear, lest, a promise being left *us* of entering into his rest, any of you should seem to come short of it.
>²For unto us was the gospel preached, as well as unto them: but the word preached did not profit them, not being mixed with faith in them that heard *it.* Hebrews 4:1-2

They looked at their circumstances and believed their circumstances, not what God said about where He was taking them. If you let your circumstances dictate your life, you have been had already. If you allow them, your circumstances are ruled by the kingdom of death, hell and destruction. If you want death, hell and destruction to bury you, then invite them into your home in the morning and have breakfast and tea with them and have a long discussion about what they are doing to you in your life, and that will be your faith.

What Job feared the most came upon him. If you believe the devil is out to get you, he will. If you believe your neighbor hates you, you have got it. If you believe no one loves you, you just bought it. If you believe God does not love you, you just bought that one too. "According to your faith, be it unto you."

>Then touched he their eyes, saying, According to your faith be it unto you. Matthew 9:29

Is your faith in hell or in heaven, above the earth or in the earth or under the earth?

The Bible says you are a new creation.

>Because the creature itself also shall be delivered from the bondage of corruption into the glorious liberty of the children of God. Romans 8:21

The Bible says,

Therefore if any man *be* in Christ, *he is* a new creature: old things are passed away; behold, all things are become new.
2 Corinthians 5:17

You are either going to believe that or you are going to trash it. You have been programmed to hate God by the world and your families. You have been programmed to hate yourself and you have been programmed to hate your brother. That is the spirit which is in the world. The Holy Spirit says that you shall love your enemy, you shall bless them that persecute you, you shall love the Lord thy God with all thy heart and all thy soul and all thy might, and you shall love your neighbor as you love yourself.

43Ye have heard that it hath been said, Thou shalt love thy neighbour, and hate thine enemy.
44But I say unto you, Love your enemies, bless them that curse you, do good to them that hate you, and pray for them which despitefully use you, and persecute you;
Matthew 5:43-44

An antichrist spirit won't let you love God or receive the love of God. It won't let you love yourself, and it won't allow you to love your enemies. Forget those who love you already. An Unloving spirit won't allow you to receive the love that is coming from someone who wants to love you. An Unloving spirit won't allow you even to receive the love that is being genuinely given. If someone comes up to you and says, "I think you are the best thing since peanut butter," you cannot look them in the eye.

In Genesis, the LORD God, *Elohiym* came down and walked with Adam and Eve in the cool of the evening. It was fellowship, conversation, relationship.

The beginning of the entrance of Unloving spirits is your separation from God, and your enemy is right there to come in and love you his way. But his love is perverted: he wants

71

you to have a miserable day; he wants you to think bad things about God; he wants you to think bad things about yourself; he wants you to think bad things about your neighbor. If you do not come up with enough bad things, he is going to help you know why you do not belong on this planet and why God does not love you and you just know everyone around you does not like you.

You know it because it is ingrained within you through your families, your mommies and daddies; you know how they loved you. Most of them loved you just like the devil did. They either ignored you or they told you they wished you had not been born or they brutally, emotionally, verbally and sexually abused you. You have been programmed to hate. You have been programmed to be rejected. The devil has programmed you to be unlovely, unacceptable, and rejected in your ancestry and you wonder why you are having a rough day.

It is time for you to be programmed to be loved. Faith comes by hearing and hearing by the Word of God. Be not just a hearer of the Word, but be a doer. You have to love yourself because God said so. "Thou shalt love the Lord thy God with all thy heart, and all thy soul, and all thy might and you shall love your neighbor as yourself. Upon this principle, all of the law and the prophets hang."

> [37]Jesus said unto him, Thou shalt love the Lord thy God with all thy heart, and with all thy soul, and with all thy mind.
> [38]This is the first and great commandment.
> [39]And the second *is* like unto it, Thou shalt love thy neighbour as thyself.
> [40]On these two commandments hang all the law and the prophets.   Matthew 22:37-40

The very thrust of the teaching of God through the law and the prophets is that you shall love the Lord thy God with all of thy heart, and all of thy soul, and all of thy might. That is spirit, soul, and body. You shall love your neighbor as you love yourself. Say, "I am going to love myself, I am going to be obedient to my Creator, and I am going to be obedient to my Father.

Father, I ask you to help me. I am going to love myself, I am going to accept myself, and if there is anything in me that is not of God, I do not hate *myself*, I hate that *thing* in me. But I realize that isn't me anyway."

Paul struggled with that in Romans 7. He said when he did the evil, it was not him doing it anyway; it was sin that dwelt within him that was doing it.

> **Now then it is no more I that do it, but sin that dwelleth in me.**   Romans 7:17

Now if there is a sin within you doing this dastardly deed through you, why are you blaming yourself? When that Bitterness comes, why don't you say, "Hey wait a minute, you aren't me, get out of here." But you don't do that. You say, "What did you say? I didn't hear that loud enough. Yeah, they didn't listen to me yesterday. No, they don't care for me; they didn't even smile at me like they used to. They're preoccupied. They probably like someone else better than me now. Yeah, I knew it. Daddy and mommy told me I was nothing anyway."

I saw a TV program once about young ladies that had been scorned and victimized in youth because they were considered to be ugly. One girl is still trying to recover herself from the pain and the scarring of her peers when she was growing up because they considered her to be, not homely, but ugly. What children do to other children and how they trash them! Competition comes in to cause them to try and measure up to someone else's scorn and Accusation.

These little girls that were ugly when they were in school are adults now and they are not ugly any more All of these girls turned out as adult women to be very attractive ladies on the outside. We do not know what they are like on the inside, spiritually or emotionally. You are not as you shall be.

You are not as you shall be, but in the twinkling of an eye, you shall be changed.

> In a moment, in the twinkling of an eye, at the last trump: for the trumpet shall sound, and the dead shall be raised incorruptible, and we shall be changed.   1 Corinthians 15:52

Well, if you are going to be changed in a twinkling of an eye in the first resurrection, why don't you start getting it together spiritually now before the first resurrection? Do you remember in the parable about the virgins? Five were called foolish and five were called wise. The five that were wise kept their vessels filled up with oil which is a type of the Holy Spirit. They were waiting for the bridegroom, filled with expectation. They knew they were chosen, they knew they were wanted, they were expectantly waiting and ready to go. When the cry went out, they were right there to receive the fruit of that relationship, but the others were having a good day, carrying on and living their life.

THE FLESH

Paul said to know no man after the flesh.

> Wherefore henceforth know we no man after the flesh...
> 2 Corinthians 5:16

That means both ways — both as a physical entity and evil spirit reality. The word "flesh" can be translated as the human body in the Greek, or it can be translated as your nature that does not match the nature of God. If there is any part of your nature that does not match the nature of God, you have been under the influence of and programmed by evil spirits in your generations, in your personal life, and right down the line. When the evil spirits are removed from your personality, what is left is you.

When the Bible says your mind is renewed by the washing of the water of the Word, it means that your mind is renewed, your thinking has been changed, your nature has been changed, and your personality has been changed.

If you read the newspapers and national magazines, they are saying the way you think affects your health.

If you want better health, change the way you think.

When they say it, they expose it as just stinkin' thinkin'. There is a spirit in the world that does not want to be exposed as an evil spirit. Paul said in Romans he wanted to change his stinkin' thinkin'; he wanted to think differently, he wanted to have a new personality, he wanted to think, speak, and act differently, but the harder he tried the behinder he got. He says, "The good that I wish that I could do, I do not do it; and the evil that I wish I would not do, that is what I do."

For the good that I would I do not: but the evil which I would not, that I do. Romans 7:19

"So in the day that I do this evil that I hate to do, it is no longer I that am doing this evil, but it is sin that dwells in me that is doing it!" Well, Paul needed a personality change. He needed a spiritual change. He needed to get it together. He needed God to deliver him of those areas of sin that were within him.

When I get to heaven, I am going to find Paul and give him the biggest hug he has ever gotten in his life. He is going to squirm because I am going to thank him for Romans 7

75

and his honesty. Romans 7 has allowed me to be free and allowed many other people to be set free through the ministry of this church.

We must see that part of us that is not us.

Do you want to be free and have a new way, a new life? Do you want to think differently? Are you tired of this stuff boiling on the inside of you? Some people enjoy being insane. Some people enjoy feeling unlovely. Some people enjoy hating themselves. The worst thing that can happen to some people is for them to get well because they would then have to serve God. When they are sick they do not have to: all they have to do is mulligrub around about their sickness and their disease.

Do you want to be well? There are three dimensions: spirit, soul and body. Thou shalt love the Lord thy God. You need to be stirred up to good works. Hebrews says,

> But exhort one another daily, while it is called To day; lest any of you be hardened through the deceitfulness of sin.
>
> Hebrews 3:13

The Bible talks about those who have itching ears and gather around teachers and preachers.

> For the time will come when they will not endure sound doctrine; but after their own lusts shall they heap to themselves teachers, having itching ears; 2 Timothy 4:3

Jeremiah says, "Guys, if you don't get it together before the Lord, you are going into captivity for 70 years." (Jeremiah 25) The other prophets in the church at that time came along and got up in the synagogue and said, "Well, Jeremiah has prophesied, but he doesn't really know the heart of God. Haven't you read that God is love and is longsuffering, and David said His mercy endureth forever; His longsuffering is in the earth. God loves you, so your captivity, yes, it is coming, but it will only be for two years, and then God's blessing will come and shadow all over you. So it is two years of punishment, not 70, thus saith the Lord."

Jeremiah said, "Well, maybe God is right, maybe I didn't hear God. Maybe I didn't hear you, God. Well, I could be wrong and they could be right, maybe I just got overbalanced here and I just got a zeal without knowledge and maybe I have divination and I prophesied 70 years and all these other people say it is two years."

Then the Bible says that Jeremiah started to leave the building because he was thinking they could be right. So the Spirit of God dropped in him and he turned around and walked back to the door and said this, "In two years you are all dead, prophets. Enjoy your two years of punishment because at the end is not prosperity, it is your personal death." Those same false prophets were taken into captivity by Nebuchadnezzar and killed.

Serving the devil is terrible. Listening to divination is terrible. Setting up the kingdom of the devil in the earth is terrible. Overthrowing the government of God in the earth is terrible. Preaching a gospel that says you do not have to obey the Word of God is terrible. Preaching a gospel that denies and defies the very written Scripture is terrible. Teaching a gospel that you do not have to love God is terrible. Teaching a gospel that you do not have to love yourself is terrible. Teaching a gospel that you do not have to love your neighbor is terrible.

All disease in the earth is here today because of the doctrine that is in the earth: you do not have to love God, you do not have to love yourself, and you do not have to love your neighbor. Yet all the *autoimmune* diseases that are out there are a result of someone not loving themselves. At least 30 or 40 percent of all *cancers* that are in mankind are there because you do not love your neighbor as yourself. There is much Bitterness and hatred. All *insanity* is there because you are separated from God and His love. Faith represents God; Fear represents the devil. In 1 John 4:18 it says that Fear hath torment. Where is that torment? Right between your ears. All insanity is rooted in separation from God and His Word and His love and because of falling under occultism at some point in life.

When it comes to the part about being reconciled to God, the beginning of unraveling all spiritually rooted disease is getting right with God, getting right with yourself and getting right with others. Getting right with God does not just mean accepting His love, you have to get the occultism out of your life.

MCS/EI stands on two legs and unless both of these legs are totally broken, there cannot be total of freedom from MCS/EI. One of these legs is Fear coming out of a broken heart and the other is occultism which means being involved in any modality of spirituality from the second heaven. In order for you to have your peace of mind from Fear, it is not just the healing of the broken heart.

You are going to have to get right with God because you have served the devil in your thinking, your religions, your philosophies, your idolatries, your superstitions and your ways that have not matched what the Word of God has said about Himself and about others.

God is not going to deny himself. "He is not a man that He should lie, nor the son of man that He should repent."

> God *is* not a man, that he should lie; neither the son of man, that he should repent: hath he said, and shall he not do it? or hath he spoken, and shall he not make it good?
>
> Numbers 23:19

"Let God be true and every man a liar."

> God forbid: yea, let God be true, but every man a liar; as it
> is written, That thou mightest be justified in thy sayings, and
> mightest overcome when thou art judged.   Romans 3:4

DOCTRINES OF DEVILS

Any modalities of spirituality that cannot be substantiated by the written Word of God are of the devil and are called doctrines of devils. What is a doctrine of devils? The New Testament tells you. "Eat no meat" is a doctrine of devils. "Do not get married" is a doctrine of devils.

> [1]Now the Spirit speaketh expressly, that in the latter times
> some shall depart from the faith, giving heed to seducing
> spirits, and doctrines of devils;
> [2]Speaking lies in hypocrisy; having their conscience
> seared with a hot iron;
> [3]Forbidding to marry, *and commanding* to abstain from
> meats, which God hath created to be received with
> thanksgiving of them which believe and know the truth.
> 1 Timothy 4:1-3

Doctrines of devils can come in many, many forms. Evil spirits can teach you through men. An antichrist spirit won't allow you to love yourself, but God has commanded you to love yourself. Thou shalt love the Lord thy God with all thy heart and with all thy soul, and all thy might, and thou shalt love thy neighbor as you love thyself. There is a commandment to accept yourself and to love yourself. An antichrist spirit won't allow you to obey the Word of God. It will look for every way out. It will try to tell you why the Word of God is not true. It will try to tell you why you do not have to listen. Why you do not have to obey.

When you find any spirit coming into your mind accusing the Word of God and the Scriptures to you, you

79

have an antichrist spirit that is working you over. Jesus said, "If you love me, you will keep the commandments." So when you do not keep the commandments of Christ, you do not love Him and you can't love yourself then because you are in rebellion against God.

ANTICHRIST SPIRIT

It is impossible for a person to really love themselves and not have a relationship with God; the peace in that would always be suspect. There is always strife. Perhaps we are dealing with fabricated personalities or we are dealing with people who are in denial, or we are dealing with people who are covering things up. The world out there is really in trouble in relationship with God, and with relationship with themselves and with relationship with others.

An antichrist spirit always brings Accusation of some form. An antichrist spirit is one who denies the Lord Jesus. An antichrist spirit is one who denies God the Father and His identity. An antichrist spirit is one who redefines the Holy Spirit in his identity. An antichrist spirit is any modality or spirituality or statement or existence or belief that changes any dimension of the Godhead and changes in any dimension what the Scriptures have said.

An antichrist spirit denies that Jesus Christ has come in the flesh. An antichrist spirit denies that Jesus is God the Word. An antichrist spirit denies that Jesus is the only way to God because He said He was. An antichrist spirit says, "This scripture is not true, I do not have to obey it, I do not have to believe it." An antichrist spirit is one that would come into any person who would keep you from obeying the Word of God. If the Bible says to forgive your enemy and you do not, an antichrist spirit is behind it.

Behind the Unloving spirit is an antichrist spirit because it refuses to let you accept the love of God and love yourself and love your neighbor. That is an antichrist spirit that is on the loose. The Bible says in 1 John 4:20 that if you say you love God and you do not love your neighbor, the love of God is not within you. You are in denial, you are in deception, and that is an antichrist spirit. An antichrist spirit produces all false religions. An antichrist spirit produces all modalities of spirituality as an attempt to get away from what God has said about the past, present and future.

Anyone who says there is no hell has an antichrist spirit because Jesus said there was a hell. Any statement that says that mankind does not have to stand in judgment one day for his sins is an antichrist spirit because the Lord Himself said they would. Anything that comes against the written Scriptures is an antichrist spirit.

There is a great observation now that people who have some form of religion — it does not even have to be God's religion — any type or form of religion, going to any kind of church service, whether it be an antichrist church or a real one, anyone who has some type of faith modality has less Fear, is less prone to anxiety and stress disorders. Faith and prayer of any type has a benefit. The Scriptures say perfect peace belongs to those whose minds are fixed or stayed on the Lord.

> **Thou wilt keep *him* in perfect peace, *whose* mind *is* stayed *on thee:* because he trusteth in thee.**   Isaiah 26:3

Perfect peace belongs to those whose minds are fixed or stayed on the Lord. So an antichrist statement would be that you do not have to keep your mind on the Lord or that you do not have to serve God. Satan knows you physiologically and psychologically better than you can imagine. There is a false peace the devil can give. There is a placebo type peace that is available to mankind and Satan not only comes in destruction, but he comes in deception. He will come and give you a spirituality and your body will respond so that your anxiety levels go down because the devil knows that if he can bring you to a place in certain types of meditations where you start to focus and to take your time and get away from that stressor, he knows that your hypothalamus will stop secreting the hormone causing the anxiety disorder. He is able to program you and control you based on giving you a benefit.

The Bible is very clear that Satan also comes as an angel of light. That is why there are teachings out there that talk about "God is love." There are organizations and religions that teach about the love of God, the love, love, love. But the god that they are offering is not the one found in Scripture. Can the devil heal? Absolutely, Jannes and Jambres did. Can psychic healing be real? If the devil and his kingdom can put an evil spirit on someone, he can take it off at his will to get them just where he wants them. You have to remember that the devil does not come just for destruction; he comes for deception to separate you from the relationship of the living God.

Corinthians says,

> 4(For the weapons of our warfare are not carnal, but mighty through God to the pulling down of strong holds;)
> 5Casting down imaginations, and every high thing that exalteth itself against the knowledge of God, and bringing into captivity every thought to the obedience of Christ;
> 2 Corinthians 10:4-5

You not only have words that form in the mind, you have pictures. There is a startling insight in 2 Corinthians 10:5. It says, "The weapons of our warfare are not carnal, but mighty to the pulling down of strongholds, holding every thought in captivity, casting down every imagination."

When I looked up the word "imagination" in the *Strong's Concordance* and *Webster's Dictionary*, there is a visual picture in the mind. You have word and picture. So you hold every thought captive and cast down every day the pictorial manifestations in your mind and hold it captive, whether it be a thought or a picture. Any modality that would try to give you a benefit that does not match the knowledge of God is antichrist. It may give you a measure of peace, but it won't give you perfect peace. Do you want a placebo peace in your life, do you want a managed peace in your life, do you want Prozac or anti-anxiety drugs, do you want some modality to give you peace or do you want perfect peace?

When you have perfect peace, you do not need to manage anything. It is your way of existence, as you are in Christ, as you are in the Father and no longer do you have to be concerned about anxiety and lack of peace, you are walking in peace. It is possible because of what Jesus said, "Peace give I unto you, but not as the world gives." Jesus said there is a peace that the world gives and then there is a peace that He gives you. The peace that Jesus gives you is a perfect peace, not a managed peace.

The antichrist spirit won't allow you to love. The antichrist spirit won't allow you to receive love. We are not talking about people who love each other and their families. There are many people who are not saved, but they love their children, love their families, and the rain falls on the just and the unjust.

The principles of God are applied by people saved and unsaved, so do not think an unsaved person cannot partake of the blessings of God. There are some unsaved people who do not have the same curses as some Christians do. To the degree that you line up with God and His Word, to that degree God will honor that in your life because His principles are eternal and He honors His Word. The Bible also says do not be too concerned when you see the ungodly prospering in the way. He shall have his end as the flower does at the end of the fall. The issue is: who gets resurrected in the spring?

The antichrist Unloving spirit promotes, number one, disobedience to God's Word (that is against relationship with God); and, number two, accepting unscriptural precepts as a way of life. Disobedience to God is of the antichrist spirit. Relationship with God would be in the area of a son or daughter of God by faith in love, in repentance, taking responsibility, but accepting scriptural precepts as a way of life. What is an unscriptural principle? What is an antichrist precept? God is going to love you, and you can hate your neighbor.

But the Bible says this, if you say you love God and you hate your neighbor, the love of God is not within you. You should forgive your neighbor. If you from your heart do not forgive your brother his trespass, your Father which is in heaven shall not forgive you yours. You cannot write your own Bible. It is antichrist. You cannot disobey the Scriptures. It is antichrist.

Not accepting and loving yourself is an antichrist spirit within you because Psalm 139:14 says that you are fearfully and wonderfully made. Before you were fashioned in the womb of your mother by the sperm and the egg, before your bones and your eyes and your hair and the rest of your body and the rest of what you are was created, God knew you.

In Psalm 17:8, He says you are the apple of His eye. Isaiah 49:16 says you are engraved on the palms of His hands. You are no accident. When He sent His Holy Spirit and saved you, that was the ultimate test of love because He died for you.

84

John says,

Greater love hath no man than this, that a man lay down his life for his friends. John 15:13

SELF-PITY

If there is an Unloving spirit within you, then Self-Pity, which is an antichrist spirit, is there also. No one is healed of Multiple Chemical Sensitivity/Environmental Illness (MCS/EI) totally unless this is gone. No one will be free of MCS/EI unless Self-Pity is broken forever. Self-Pity is bad news. It is an evil spirit that will cause you to look inward at yourself and will bind you to the past.

When projecting to the future, Self-Pity tells you that no one really cares and they really do not understand what you are going through. If they did, they would be on your doorstep 24 hours a day, loving on you, laughing with you, taking care of you. It tells you that everyone is insensitive around you. It tells you that they only care about themselves. It tells you that you are unlovely and you know it. In ministry, if we start to stir up Self-Pity, we become an instant enemy to you. You won't be able to easily separate yourself from this thought, this emotion and this feeling.

When Jesus was on the cross, He was not in Self-Pity. When He was on the cross dying for your sins and my sins, He was forgiving them for what they had done to Him, saying, "Father forgive them, they know not what they are doing." If you are going to be free of Self-Pity, concerning the people who damaged you, whether it be husband or wife, father, mother, brother, sister, friend or foe, you are going to have to say, "Father, forgive them because they *knew* not what they *were* doing."

What are you saying? They are insane spiritually, and they could not help themselves. So you take that great

85

hatred and Self-Pity and exchange it for compassion as Jesus did for us. He had been physically brutalized with a crown of thorns and blood streaming down His face and pain wracking His body, as He hung with nails driven through Him, so that you would not recognize He was a human being. On the cross when He was dying, Jesus was saying, "Father, forgive them." In His dying moments He led someone into Paradise, and He was still preaching salvation. He was thinking about those who had crucified Him and their own salvation. To the thief on the cross He said, "This day you shall be in Paradise with Me." He was still preaching the salvation message.

As Jesus was dying, He was not thinking of Himself, He was thinking of the person next to Him. He was saying to John, "Behold thy mother." He was thinking about Mary, His mother, and saying to His beloved friend John, "Take care of Mary. Treat her like your own mother. Behold your mother."

Self-Pity is an evil spirit, not an emotion. Self-Pity is not an emotion, it is an evil spirit. If you do not think so, confront it in ministry and see what happens. There was someone who had come to be healed, and we were dealing with her life. We told her at that time we were going to go after a spirit in her, and it was an evil spirit called Self-Pity. We told her when we touched it and it surfaced, she would think we were Satan himself, she would say so, and she would say that we were the devil.

She would also say that we did not care about her, that we hated her, and she would accuse us and demand to leave and go back where she came from, that she had to get away from us because we are the enemy. We warned her when this spirit surfaced, it would attack this ministry, my staff and me and her chances of surviving it and staying were not very good. It was a spirit of Self-Pity.

She said in her great faith of the moment when we told her that, "Oh that won't happen." Besides, we had a lady who was part of the ministry team and weighed about 350 pounds. She said, "If I start to do that and leave here, I give permission to have her stop me at the door and sit on me." Well, you know that would not happen, but that was her faith. So we explained to her what Self-Pity was like.

The day she came for ministry, she had a little hard-covered Bible with the cover wrapped totally in tin foil because she was still allergic to the ink and the pages. When we touched Self-Pity, all her good intentions and good faith towards us were gone.

She got up and started to attack us, "You are of the devil. You don't care for me. You don't love me. You hate me. You are evil. I should never have come here. I'm out of here. I'm on a plane. I want to be taken to the airport now. I am leaving and you are evil and if you loved me you wouldn't talk to me this way. If you loved me you wouldn't make me feel this way on the inside."

If she was feeling that way on the inside, and we were on the outside, where was that coming from? The evil spirit of Self-Pity. She stood up and she said, "You are the devil. You are Satan himself. I am out of here. I never should have come to this place." She stood up, spouting this stuff off and then she stopped, reached over and grabbed that foil-lined Bible, held it right to her chest and planted her feet.

From that point, we did not say anything; we just sat back and stared at her. She took that spirit on herself and she said, "Wait a minute, they warned me about you. You are Self-Pity, and they said you would say these things through me. These are lovely people, they aren't of the devil. They've been laying their life down for me, Self-Pity, I take authority over you and you are not going to destroy me. You are not going to rip me off and you are not going to lie about these people. They are of God. Now you get out of me in the name of Jesus Christ; you get out of me. You leave me."

That spirit was gone and we did nothing more. When she confronted it, it was over with. You are going to have to be prepared to confront your enemy because if you don't, you have an antichrist spirit that won't let you. John says,

> **If the Son therefore shall make you free, ye shall be free indeed.**　　　　　　　　　　　　　　　　John 8:36

There was another lady who had two children aged 3 and 5 and they all had EI. I flew with my team across America for five days to help this family. The husband picked us up at the airport and it was a two-hour drive home. I told the husband, "I need to prep you on some things. I appreciate a husband being involved in his wife's freedom, but I am going to have to give you some facts of life."

So we stopped at a restaurant to get a bite to eat. I explained to him what we were dealing with and what we hoped to accomplish in five days. It would be morning, afternoon, and night; it would be "round the clock" ministry except for some time for sleep and a bite to eat.

It would be head-to-head confrontation. I remember saying this to him, "About two or three days into this, we are going to touch an evil spirit in your wife called Self-Pity. We are going to build a case against your wife's enemy to get her free of this disease and at one stage in the ministry when we touch Self-Pity; I am going to become Satan himself to her. She is going to demand you remove us from your home, and she is going to demand we be put on a plane out of here and that my ministry is of the devil and I am of the devil and that I am abusive. She will demand you remove me and my team from this home."

He said, "You are kidding? That is pretty serious." I said, "Self-Pity is that dangerous. Now I am going to forewarn you and I am going to tell you the very words she will say so that when she says them, you will know that I know what I am talking about and I have already forewarned you what she will say. It will not be her speaking; it will be the evil spirit of Self-Pity from the past that is binding her to this disease.

Unless that is gone and defeated, she will never be healed totally of MCS/EI. She may have a better life, but she will never be totally healed while Self-Pity is there." He said, "That's pretty tough, but I hear you."

We got into ministry and about the third day, we got up and came downstairs. Later I found out she had been up since three, and she had been bending his ear. I came down about 7:30 to get a little cereal. She was already downstairs sitting on the couch. She did not say good morning, and she was not friendly. She was sitting there with a black cloud all over her face, and I knew we were ready to confront Self-Pity.

I looked at the husband and said, "Can I have a word with you." We went out, and he said, "If you hadn't told me this, I wouldn't have believed it because you are asking me to make a choice between you and my wife. My wife has asked me to remove you immediately and put you on a plane because you are of the devil. She says you are insensitive to her, and you are evil. She says if you really cared for her, you would not be so confrontational and you would act like you really cared for her. But all you have been doing is confronting her and confronting her issues, and she does not want you to stay. She said you are of the devil, that your ministry is evil and so are you and you have to leave the home immediately."

I said, "Where are you in this? When I go back in that room, I am going to take Self-Pity on for size. It is here. Now where are you in it?" He said, "If you hadn't told me, I would be on her side because she is my wife. But you told me and she said word-for-word what you said she would say." But she did not know that because he did not tell her. I did not tell her anything. He said, "I am going with you." I said, "She is going to demand you remove us." He said, "Yes, I know she is." I said, "Are you ready for this kind of war?" He said, "Let's go for it." I said, "Okay."

We walked back in the room and she started to spout, "Get out of here. You are Satan. You are evil." She called him by his first name and said, "Get them out of this home. Get them back to the airport and get them out of here, now! I command you to get these people out of my house."

But that husband was strong, and he said, "No, these people are of God. They've come to set you free. Self-Pity is up and everything you have told me in the bedroom at 3:00 and 4:00, he warned me three days ago that you would say it and you have said it. I know he is telling me the truth. They are staying!"

We went to war, and I took that Self-Pity spirit on, I scorned it. When I scorn Self-Pity, you think I am scorning you. I do not have any patience for it, and I will say all the things that it is saying to you inside your mind. Every word I say will be its words. If you do not know, you think I am taking you on for size. I am taking on that antichrist spirit of Self-Pity that is trying to bind you to your disease and take you back to the past saying, "No, I am not loved." Self-Pity will tell you that you are not loved! Self-Pity will tell you

90

that no one understands and no one cares! That is what it will tell you.

So I got a little stool and pulled it up next to the couch, and in the name of Jesus Christ of Nazareth, I came against that foul, unclean spirit of Self-Pity. She rolled up against the couch and turned her face from me and put her hands over her ears. First of all she could not intimidate me, and she could not intimidate her husband because we were going nowhere.

So that did not work. She rolled over against the couch and put her hands over her ears and I simply said this, "Evil spirit, you are not a physical entity, and you can hear me well. So I am going to speak to you, and her holding her hands over her ears means nothing to me. You can hear me and you are going."

I took that thing on for size and in about five or ten minutes it was over with. That spirit came out of her and she rolled over from the sofa and looked at me with a big smile on her face and said, "I have never felt so good. How are you doing, Pastor? I am so glad you stayed through this one." All of a sudden I am a friend again. Within two days she was totally freed of MCS/EI as were both of her children. In five days we left and that family is well today.

SEPARATE YOURSELF FROM THE ANTICHRIST SPIRIT

You must separate yourself from the antichrist spirit in you that is not really you. Your issues must be confronted. If you do not love yourself, the spirit within you is antichrist and is keeping you from being obedient to Christ, because He loves you. He has accepted you and in the metaphorical sense He wants to walk with you in the cool of the evening.

In Revelation it tells you what He wants to do (this is not for the unsaved, this is for the saved). These are the words of Jesus Christ Himself to John the Revelator to the church and you are a member of the church today. "As many as I love, I rebuke and chasten."

> ¹⁹As many as I love, I rebuke and chasten: be zealous therefore, and repent.
> ²⁰Behold, I stand at the door, and knock: if any man hear my voice, and open the door, I will come in to him, and will sup with him, and he with me.
>
> Revelation 3:19-20

You must deal with your life issues. You must repent, get it together and listen. Everything we teach you can be found in Scripture. Everything we teach you is birthed by the Spirit of God and confirmed by the Word of God, hopefully always with love. We have a heart for you like you would never believe. That same Spirit that delivered us (me and my staff) is the same Spirit that will deliver you — The Spirit of the living God.

You must confront the issues of your life that you have never been able to confront before. If you do not, you cannot be free with this stuff on the inside of you that accuses you to yourself, accuses you to others, and accuses you to God. You must remove that antichrist thinking from your mind and decide to accept yourself once and for all. When you surface making growling noises, that is not you. We are able to separate you from that. So when that thing is gone which has become one with you, one with your thinking, one with your speech, and one with your action, we can then have our fellowship together.

The Unloving spirit is one of the toughest areas to go because it touches the core of every person. The number one bondage of the devil is self-hatred and self-rejection. Self-Hatred and self-rejection are strong underlings of the

Unloving spirit, which is one of the strongest evil principalities in mankind. (It makes you feel so yucky about yourself.)

Self-Pity also has to be dealt with. In Revelation 3:19, Jesus said, "As many as I love, I rebuke and chasten. Be zealous therefore and repent." Why does Jesus rebuke you and chasten you? "Behold I stand at the door and knock (at your heart's door). If any man hear my voice and open the door, I will come in to him and I will sup with him and he with me." There is the fellowship. There is the relationship. There it is. What do the Lord and the Father want to do with you today? They want a relationship with you. I want you to be in fellowship with God, but if you, like Adam and Eve, go and hide in the bushes, what is He going to do?

The Unloving spirit separates you from the love of God.

Self-Pity will separate you from the love of God. Do you want to experience the love of God? Then you are going to have to get the Unloving spirit out of you because the Unloving spirit won't allow you to receive the love of God. If you can't receive the love of God, you can't receive the love of others. It is impossible.

If you do not understand what made other people evil towards you and are not able to separate them from their evil and exchange Bitterness for compassion, we are not going anywhere because you have an antichrist spirit. Why would you have an antichrist spirit? Because Jesus is the Christ, and He forgave them on the cross and He saved them even at death.

If you are after the Spirit of God, you will be just like your Savior. Jesus knew He would die on the cross before He went there, and He knew before He came from heaven and was made incarnate in the womb of Mary. The Bible says in Jeremiah 51:40 that we are like lambs led to the slaughter. Self-Pity won't let you go to the slaughter. We are killed all the day long. Self-Pity won't let you go there. It won't let you be vulnerable. It will insist that there be no problems, that everyone be holy next to God Himself on the throne and that you will never have another problem or an attack by anyone the rest of your life.

Self-Pity won't let you go there. Self-Pity won't let you be vulnerable. Self-Pity won't let you be you. Revelation 12:11 says they overcame Satan by the blood of the Lamb and by the word of their testimony and they loved not their life even to the death.

THE KINGDOM OF SELF

Self-Pity produces another dimension of the Unloving spirit called the kingdom of Self. You are now your own god. The sun shall rise and set on your perceptions. *Self, self, self, me, me, me, my, my, my. My* realities, *my* perceptions, *my* disease, *my* pain, *my* theology, *my* decision about what is right or wrong, and *my* decision whether I am going to be obedient or not. What *I* decide today is the way *I* am going to be. The kingdom of Self then begins with the kingdom of something called self-introspection. Inversion, looking in, and looking inward.

The Bible says,

> **And when these things begin to come to pass, then look up, and lift up your heads; for your redemption draweth nigh.** Luke 21:28

Lift up those feeble hands that hang down.

> **Wherefore lift up the hands which hang down, and the feeble knees;** Hebrews 12:12

Look out, lift up, put on the garment of praise, remove the spirit of heaviness, accept God's love, love yourself, love your neighbor, and when they are killing you, forgive them and save their souls. There is a mentality that you are only going to represent God and save those who are nice to you. Do you want to be like your Father in heaven? You were created from the foundation of the world in His image. So in whose image are you? You cannot love your neighbor if you do not love yourself; it is impossible. You are going to have to receive that you are important and that you are loved of God. When you do not love yourself, you are calling God a liar and that is an antichrist spirit, a lying spirit that refuses for you to be able to accept yourself.

PRIDE

Pride is an antichrist mentality. Another form of pride is saying that you are nothing. Have you ever seen anyone that has false humility? An example is when a person says, "I am sorry, the Bible says I am to prefer others above myself so you just go right ahead." That is pride. Pride is not just someone exalting himself; pride is someone who is debasing himself also; it is false pride. It is still self-centeredness and building oneself up.

In Job 41:34, Leviathan is called the father of the children of pride. With respect to an Unloving spirit, pride won't let a person be honest with himself. Pride will say everyone else has the problem, but I don't have it. Pride will never take responsibility for obedience to the Word of God. Pride will never be in submission to leadership, even God or the five-fold ministry in the local church. Pride never takes responsibility for error. Pride never repents and never admits it is wrong. Pride never, never, never, never takes responsibility for anything. It is Luciferian and exalts itself totally.

MIND-BODY CONNECTION

Now, understanding the mind-body connection, we know there is a direct relationship between how we think and our physiology. When we study Fear, anxiety and stress we find out that there is a direct connection between the hypothalamus, the endocrine system, and the sympathetic nervous system. People who have this type of disobedience to God, not accepting and loving yourself, and have a kingdom of Self, are prone to pain because the neurological processes are responding to it.

The Unloving spirit produces pain.

The Unloving spirit produces pain of the spirit. Self-Rejection and self-hatred produce the deepest pain known to man. An Unloving spirit produces the deepest, deepest breaking of the human spirit. Neurologically and spiritually you are in pain from an Unloving spirit. When you have Self-Pity, you have massive amounts of psychogenic pain. Psychogenic pain comes from the root word *psycho*, meaning soul. It is pain that has no organic reason, nor is there really a problem. But there is pain. It can be in the spine or in the muscles.

Fibromyalgia is a psychogenic type of pain. There is nothing wrong in the muscles or the ligaments, or the tendons or the white connective tissue of the body. There is nothing wrong. When a person is suffering from fibromyalgia, organically there is nothing wrong with them, but the pain they are having is very real. The pain is coming from Fear, anxiety and stress, causing the sympathetic nervous system to initiate a nerve impulse down the nerve to the various parts of the body that are localized, systemic or generalized. The nerve impulse goes into the end of the dendrite and just sits there pulsating with no corresponding action required. Fibromyalgia is a psychogenic-type pain.

How many more pains do you have coming out of the conflict of the soul?

An antichrist spirit will always produce pain. Many people are dealing with spinal cord pain that is coming out of an antichrist, Unloving spirit that includes separation from God. Many people in occultism have many types of tormenting pain. Pain comes with the breaking of the heart, the kingdom of Self. When you start to concentrate on your spiritual and soulish and biological processes and you become so inverted that all you can see is yourself, then your body responds accordingly and you have a manifestation of self.

Self-Pity is a killer when it comes to damaging and producing psychogenic pain. Self-Pity amplifies every thought; Self-Pity says no one cares about you; Self-Pity says no one understands what you have been through; Self-Pity says everyone is insensitive to you. Self-Pity says you know you are the worm, and everyone knows it. Self-Pity will always bind you to the past and remind you of your failures and the failures of everyone concerning you, and then it comes with something called imaginations.

It will paint you picture, after picture, after picture in your mind, and it will wake you at night in torment. It will send the night tormenter to you because the Unloving spirit is the open door. Introspection, inversion, the kingdom of Self, me, my, me, my own, me, me, me, me... The pictures are constantly being flashed. Those thoughts and those pictures have the ability to affect you in all dimensions.

The Unloving spirit has to go. Fear will tell you it is not going to happen. But when you have seen one poor devil, you have seen them all. They are so uncreative. They are so boring. They are like pushing a play button on a tape machine. One person pushes the right button, zap; the next

97

person comes along and pushes the right button, zap, word-for-word. They say the same things They do the same things. They are so boring. One of the things an evil spirit will say when is it being dealt with is "I am not going, I am staying right here. Sorry, I know you cast me out in the name of Jesus, but I am staying. I am not going anywhere." Then you come along and you say, "I agree" and you let it stay.

You have to be prepared to take your life back. If you are expecting me and God and my staff to come in and do this against your will, you can forget it. If you think we can do anything more for you than you are already allowing God to do for you, you can forget it. You are going to have to be ready to fight to be free. Resist the devil and he shall flee.

Self-Pity will say to you, "That's nice, it was good for those two ladies that you talked about; that was so neat, but for me it is not going to work." That is Self-Pity. "I'm not spiritual enough. Besides, there are others more deserving than me." That is reverse pride. "There are others more deserving to be free than me and besides someone needs to carry the cross of the Savior. It might as well be me."

"Someone needs to be an oracle for the devil and I am very good at that. I have been doing it for 30 years. I want to be free, but someone's got to make this statement." When you minister to people, you hear the same old, same old. They always tell you why they cannot be free. They always tell you why they can't be delivered. They are always giving you reasons why it is not going to work for them. That is coming out of the Unloving spirit. That is coming out of Self-Pity. Self-Pity will demand you stay tormented and sick. It only looks at itself and its own realities.

When Self-Pity is gone and self is dying, you are saving someone. When Self-Pity is gone, you take no thought for your own life and what is going on in it. Your life is not your own anymore. You are hidden in Christ. In that there is great freedom and great victory.

But Self-Pity, that Unloving spirit, won't allow you even to speculate on that kind of freedom because it takes all the issues of your life, and through thoughts and vain imaginations, keeps projecting to you. Then pride comes along and justifies it. Well, this is the way I am because of this reason. "Yes, I love what you are saying. Oh my heart rejoices, glory to God, yes, Jesus" but in your heart you are saying, "But this is not for me. This is not for me." Or in your heart you are saying, "But if daddy had not said or done that to me, I would be able to walk in this. Or if mommy had not said or done this to me, I would be able to believe. But what mommy or daddy said or did to me, I just can't get over it, and it torments me day and night."

That is an antichrist, Unloving spirit. That is Self-Pity. That is self-rejection; that is self-hatred. In fact, you are making your mommy and your daddy, or your husband or your wife, or whoever it might be, you are making them your god and their word greater than the Word of God. That puts you in idolatry to your parents and, in fact, makes Satan your father all over again. I do not care if you are born again or not, in that area Satan is your lord because you believe the word of someone who abused you over the Word of the Lord who died for you to save you and redeem you and to heal you and deliver you. Your inability to walk in God is an antichrist spirit of unbelief and doubt and Fear.

WHOSE REPORT WILL YOU BELIEVE?

There is nothing better than being free. He whom the Son makes free, is free indeed. **"Keep in mind, I am not what I** was, and I am not what I am going to be. I am in a state of change."

Everything you are in your thinking is because you have been exposed to something. The compositeness of who you are, in your realities, the intellectual part of you, the spiritual part of you, is the product of your past. You have either been taught something by someone or you have been exposed to something through someone. You have recorded all of these words, images, visions and realities in your little recorder called your mind or your brain or your memory.

Those things recorded there may influence you today. That includes Rejection, Bitterness, Envy and Jealousy... Do you find yourself casting certain things down that come into your thinking every day? Do you find yourself learning how to weigh and consider? Or do you just go follow your brain cells when there's a thought and run with it? Do you build distance between your brain thought and your tongue or your action? We need to. That is wisdom.

You can have all the knowledge in the world, but you still need wisdom. Knowledge is a tool you work with, but wisdom is the measure of time in which you evaluate and allow God to get involved. The Holy Spirit operates in wisdom according to knowledge. Sometimes we do not give the Holy Spirit a chance to work with us. We are so acclimated to going from point A to point Z because of past memes, past action, past thought, or past responses. You can have Rejection so ingrained in you that if anyone says a wrong thing, you can be in a rage instantly. You can go from point A to point Z in a moment because you have been conditioned to do so. Have you ever been delivered of something and you know it, but it took you awhile to work it out? The Bible says in Philippians 2:12 to work out your own salvation daily, so there is work involved.

Many people say, "Well, I just want to be delivered." "Well, what do you want to be delivered from?" "Well, I do not care, just get on with it; let's just get it all out." It is not that easy because you have to participate. "You act and God reacts." If you are waiting for God to act, thinking then you will react, you are wasting your time, He already has.

He came and died for you, He gave you His Word, He gave you the Holy Spirit, He gave you all the knowledge you need to know about the past, present, and future. He has already done everything for you. What more do you want Him to do? Do you want Him to fix you? He already has, in His heart. When Jesus said it was finished, it was finished. Now, it is something you appropriate into your life every single day. Do you appropriate things? You have to understand there is an action required on your part.

Those feelings that come over you come quickly and fast. You can stagger and go down under those thoughts, those feelings and those emotions. It may be a day before you surface. By that time, the dastardly deeds of the devil have been completed, and you are picking up the mess and the shambles.

You know when you have blown it. Why don't we have our nature changed to the point we already are prepared to walk in forgiveness, not to go into Rejection, not to have Envy and Jealousy, not to feel unloved? Why don't we have that completeness within us that we just know who we are? I think that requires some effort. This scripture reflects a condition in the Word.

> **But seek ye first the kingdom of God, and his righteousness; and all these things shall be added unto you.**
> Matthew 6:33

God is going to give to you on the basis of your ability to handle it. The Bible says in 1 Timothy 3:6 that you should not appoint a novice to be a ruler in the church of Christ, lest he be puffed up in vanity and pride. That means there is a measure of time in which God perfects Himself within you and then He can trust you with creation. Can God trust you with creation? If God gave you 1,000 people to care for and none were saints, what would you do with them? None of them had it together: all of them had festering sores, and all of them were hurting. What would you do with them?

Grow faster by helping other people.

You can grow up faster by helping people than by any other method. The same thing I have to give to you, I have to make that thing part of my life so I get to grow up with you too. I get to apply the principles to my life every single day. You are the product of your past, and that is unfortunate because a lot of it had nothing to do with God and His will for you. If you continue to pattern your future on the basis of your past, you will have the fruit of your past. That is not God's will for you either.

It is time for you to make a decision that you are going to believe God. You are going to accept His love, you are going to believe His Word, and you are going to apply it to your life, whether you feel like it or not. You would be walking by faith because the evidence that faith stands for has yet to come to pass. If you are practicing loving your neighbor, that does not make you a hypocrite; it means you are practicing and putting into application the part of your nature that should have been there from the beginning. You are casting down imaginations. Many of us, instead of being educated by our parents to be love receivers, were conditioned by our parents to be hate receivers.

The desolation of the family is the root of all disease in the world today. If the family could be restored, the church could be restored. If the church could be restored, the city could be restored. If the city could be restored, the state could be restored. If the state could be restored, the country could be restored. If the country could be restored, the world could be restored. That won't happen until the Prince of Peace comes. That won't happen until Jesus Christ reigns out of Jerusalem with the saints because mankind is not seeking the kingdom of God. Man is not seeking what God has said about things. Man is seeking what man said about things.

In dealing with the Unloving spirit within you, you are going to have to cast down every thought and every feeling that tells you that you are not special. You are going to have to accept yourself whether you like it or not. Why don't you dress up in godliness and niceness today? Why don't you put on the garments of righteousness? Why don't you believe you are the righteousness of God through Christ Jesus by faith?

Why don't you dress up in your righteousness? Why don't you dress up in your loveliness? Why don't you dress up in who you are really? Look at yourself and say, "You know, I am the righteousness of God through Jesus Christ by faith." That does not mean you are stuck on yourself; that does not mean you are in pride. That means you are now appreciative of who you are and what God has done for you through Jesus Christ. One of the great scriptures that makes people free is Galatians 3:28. It says that through Jesus Christ in the New Testament church, there is neither male nor female, bond nor free, Jew nor Greek. That means we are all equal.

Matthew 11:11 says of women, there is none greater born than John the Baptist, but he who is least in the kingdom of God is greater than John the Baptist. If you are in the kingdom of God, and if you are applying the principles of God, His nature, and His righteousness to your life and your nature is being changed from glory to glory, and you are the least, then you are greater than John the Baptist. John the Baptist never followed Jesus; he proclaimed Him, but never followed Him.

Well, maybe we need to be careful that we are not so busy proclaiming Christ that we forget to follow Him and His precepts. Obedience is better than sacrifice. You can get up and you can raise your hands and say, "Oh, God I love you, I love my neighbor and I am glad that I do not have as much garbage in my spiritual life as she does." You can compare yourself to others, but if you are not obedient to the Word of God yourself, then that is hypocrisy. It is not hypocrisy if you are working out your own salvation daily by faith. Hypocrisy is seeing this problem in other people, but not dealing with it in your own life. That is the leaven of the Pharisees; "Do as I say and let me do what I want."

The Bible says that your minds are renewed:

> ...by the washing of regeneration, and renewing of the Holy Ghost;
> Titus 3:5

Truth is not relative; truth is not leavened. There is no such thing as situational truth or situational ethics. There is an absolute ethic, and there is an absolute truth. That is what you need to seek. Truth is not by definition; truth is by declaration. God has declared what truth is, and we have it written down.

The cleansing of truth

Many of the ingredients to the Unloving spirit have come out of your ancestry, out of your relationships with a spouse who was abusive to you, out of parents who were abusive to you, out of a grandparent who was abusive to you, out of anyone who failed you and trashed you, telling you that you were no good. They said you were less than beautiful, and all the other words that would come to proclaim that. You have made that part of your existence. You are acting out someone else's declaration for you. An Unloving spirit of self-rejection and self-hatred will cause you to remember the words someone said to you in the past and will demand that you conform to that word.

Self-Rejection demands that you conform to the words of someone who victimized you.

It will demand that you follow the precepts of that victimization and that devastation and that lie. It will fill your mind, your emotions and your feelings with thoughts and pictures that you are no good, you never will be any good, and it is the worst thing in the world that you were ever born. Parents have told children that if I had my druthers, I would have had an abortion rather than have you. The spirit that comes into that individual is an Unloving, unclean spirit and it is there to reinforce the words of another and demand those words be fulfilled in that person's life. If you are not careful, you will follow the word of that person who did not bless you in creation, and it will demand that you measure up to its image.

Whose report are you going to believe? I shall believe the report of the Lord. Or will you believe the report of the man or the woman or the mother or the father? I have made up my mind. I staggered for 20 years of my life under the curse of a father's mouth. The day I believed God, believed that I was created from the foundation of the world by God and that I was loved by God, the day I got hold of that and God came into my heart, I *listened* to God from then on. What a change in my life when that happened!

What a shame it would be to creation if you continued to follow the visions and the words of others concerning your life and go down under them in devastation and in horror.

105

What a waste to creation to follow the words of someone who was set over you to establish you before God and to make sure you were covered as God would cover you and didn't. Maybe you have not been covered by anyone, and that is demanding to be fulfilled over and over and over again.

It is time for you to make a quality decision that you belong here, and that you are important. Acts 10:34 says, "God is no respecter of persons." What He has done for one, He will do for another. You no longer have to perform for anyone, you no longer have to go down under the hand or the voice of anyone; you are a freewill agent, sovereign in your creation. The only thing you are in subjection to is the godly theocracy of the kingdom of God, to the leadership of the kingdom of God under the authority of Jesus Christ as an extension of the Father and as a work of the Holy Spirit. You have to get to a place where you go before God and tell Him you're sorry for listening to lies.

You need to tell the devil, "Let God be true and every man a liar." (Romans 3:4) "Resist the devil and he shall flee." (James 4:7) You know that does not necessarily mean that it is Satan himself, but it is a member of his kingdom, it is a principality, it is a power, it is an evil spirit. Those things are a part of you and are around you and are in others.

What do you do? Do you sit back and have a tea party with the enemy? Do you get up in the morning and say, "Well, hello Spirit of Unloveliness. I have been waiting for you. No I did not have a good night sleep, thanks to you, but what do you have to say to me today? I know that is true. I am a loser. Yes, I am getting old. Thank you for reminding me. Yes, I know she is prettier than I am. Yes, I know I can't afford to go to Saks Fifth Avenue to buy my clothes. I see that label over there. Yes, I know that sometime today someone is going to ignore me, and thank you for giving that word of knowledge. It is going to be who? No, she is my best friend. She is going to ignore me? Well, thank you, Unloving spirit, for that word of prophetic knowledge. I will keep my eyes open all day on her to make sure I can catch her doing it." All day you know that person's going to reject you and do you know what? They can't win! Neither can you!

Whose voice are you following? The Bible says that we follow the voice of the Shepherd, and another voice we will not follow. John 10 says,

> [1]Verily, verily, I say unto you, He that entereth not by the door into the sheepfold, but climbeth up some other way, the same is a thief and a robber.
>
> [2]But he that entereth in by the door is the shepherd of the sheep.
>
> [3]To him the porter openeth; and the sheep hear his voice: and he calleth his own sheep by name, and leadeth them out.
>
> [4]And when he putteth forth his own sheep, he goeth before them, and the sheep follow him: for they know his voice.
>
> [5]And a stranger will they not follow, but will flee from him: for they know not the voice of strangers.
>
> [6]This parable spake Jesus unto them: but they understood not what things they were which he spake unto them.
>
> [7]Then said Jesus unto them again, Verily, verily, I say unto you, I am the door of the sheep.
>
> [8]All that ever came before me are thieves and robbers: but the sheep did not hear them.
>
> [9]I am the door: by me if any man enter in, he shall be saved, and shall go in and out, and find pasture.
>
> [10]The thief cometh not, but for to steal, and to kill, and to destroy: I am come that they might have life, and that they might have *it* more abundantly.
>
> [11]I am the good shepherd: the good shepherd giveth his life for the sheep.
>
> [12]But he that is an hireling, and not the shepherd, whose own the sheep are not, seeth the wolf coming, and leaveth the sheep, and fleeth: and the wolf catcheth them, and scattereth the sheep.

¹³The hireling fleeth, because he is an hireling, and careth not for the sheep.

¹⁴I am the good shepherd, and know my sheep, and am known of mine.

¹⁵As the Father knoweth me, even so know I the Father: and I lay down my life for the sheep.   John 10:1-15

The point is this: whose voice are you following? If you continue to listen to these voices within your consciousness and these emotional images and feelings, projections and imaginations that reflect the past that have made you a victim in the area of being special, cared for, loved, if you continue to follow those voices, you are following the voice of the thief. "The thief comes to kill, to steal and destroy."

Jesus said you are His sheep and He knows you by name. When you are born again, your name is written down in heaven.

Likewise, I say unto you, there is joy in the presence of the angels of God over one sinner that repenteth.   Luke 15:10

Notwithstanding in this rejoice not, that the spirits are subject unto you; but rather rejoice, because your names are written in heaven.   Luke 10:20

You are known by your name. God does not say, "Hey you." He calls you by name.

When Samuel was a little boy, and the Lord called unto him and started to appear to him to make him the great prophet that he became, what did the Lord say? He said "Samuel, hey Samuel, time to wake up." Samuel got up and went over to Eli and said, "Did you call me sir?" "No Samuel, go back to bed." "Alright, sir." He goes back to bed and this voice comes, "Samuel, Samuel." He gets up and runs over to Eli the priest and says, "Did you call me sir?" "No, no, go back to bed son, I didn't call you." About the third time, Eli said, "I think it might be the Lord speaking to you, because it sure is not me. So the next time you hear your name, son, say, 'here I am Lord' and see what happens." He went back to bed and thought, "Hmm, it might be the Lord." Here came the voice, "Samuel, Samuel." What did Samuel say? "Here I am Lord."

When Jesus appeared to Saul, who became Paul the great apostle, did Jesus call him by name? He said, "Saul, Saul, why persecuteth thou me?" You are that important. In victimization and in abuse in our families, we become no-names. Our name is not even important because if it were, then we would feel good about our name. Many people do not feel good about their name because their name was used in conjunction with abuse.

I have a small daughter who, when I ask her name several times a week, tells me; then I say to her, "I like your name. I like your name." I am reinforcing her identity. I am reinforcing the beauty of who she is. I am reinforcing her femininity. I am reinforcing her reality as a female. I am reinforcing her whole foundation to be able to be a woman of God. I keep building her up. It does not mean we do not have discipline. It does not mean we do not have to deal with things. But she knows that I love her name.

You say, "Well I don't like my name." That is your name. God will change it one day because in Revelation it says He is going to give you a new name, a name only you and He know. We are the mystical bride of Christ. When you have the right kind of marriage and you have that kind of really solid relationship, the couple has a little pet name for themselves. It is a special name, an endearment name that they use with each other that no one else knows. But this is that place of relationship. It is that place of fellowship. It is that place of importance.

Jesus is your Shepherd. He is the Word of God. The words written by men by the Holy Spirit here in the Hebrew Scriptures and the Greek are the very written concepts and information the Godhead wanted you to have. When you read Matthew, Mark, Luke, and John, Jesus Himself quoted the Hebrew Scriptures over and over and over again. He was authenticating the authenticity of the Word of God because He is the Word of God. When you read these scriptures written by the Holy Spirit, the Scriptures say that holy men wrote as they were moved by the Holy Ghost. These are words, but when you understand Jesus is the Word and you mix it with your faith, the words on these pages are life because they are God the Word and all that He wanted you to know about anything in this dispensation.

So if the Word says that you are the apple of His eye, do you say "Praise God?" Do you accept it? Do you feel special? If you do not feel special, you have an antichrist spirit because it is defying what Jesus and the Father said about you and it is calling the Father and Jesus a liar. What the antichrist, Unloving spirit will tell you is, "That is true for the person next to you, but is not true for you." It will give you 40,796 different images and pictures and words from the past to reinforce it. True or false? You have to cast down images in your life that contradict the Word of God and what He said about you.

You must know who you are in Christ. You are part of the kingdom of kings and priests in the making and you are on probation. God is perfecting you for the future forever. God loves you. You are not of the old world, but you are a new creation, a new creature in Christ Jesus. Old things have passed away and behold all things become new. You are not the image of Satan and his devastation in your life. You have been programmed to be unlovely and that is an antichrist, evil mentality. I want to give you back to God the way He

110

wanted you from the beginning and I do not care how young you are or how old you are, it can begin at any moment.

Say:

This is the first day of the rest of my life.

God let it be a new day and let me have a new life. Old things are past away and behold all things are become new. I am only going to follow the voice of the great Shepherd, and believe what He said about me. Another voice I am not going to follow. Jesus said that other voice was the thief. That voice is a hireling, who does not care for me. When trouble comes he will run and leave me abandoned and leave me devastated and not protect me. Not only that, the thief and the hireling were sent to kill, steal and destroy me. So I am not going to follow that voice ever again.

Now every negative thought that comes to your mind is the voice of the hireling and the thief. Every voice that comes into you, every thought, every picture, every imagination, as that video camera plays the picture back at you from the past, every image, every thought, everything that comes that does not tell you that you are the apple of God's eye, that you are loved and that you are the best thing since peanut butter, and that you are here by ordination in spite of sin and in spite of the sin of your ancestors, that you are beloved of God and that you are accepted of God and the congregation of the saints — every voice and every imagination that comes to you is from the thief. Whose report will you believe? I shall believe the report of the Lord.

Why am I going to believe the report of the Lord? Because He is the Creator! Jesus Christ is the Creator of all things. God created all things through Jesus Christ in His preincarnate state as God the Word. Read Hebrews 1,

Colossians 1, John 1, Genesis 1, Isaiah 42, 45 and 48. Why would I want to follow the voice of one who would want to destroy what the Creator created for Himself? In Revelation 4:11, John the Revelator says you have been created for God's pleasure. We should give our families back to God for His pleasure and make sure they know about God, and make sure they know they are loved and beloved, and teach them about discernment in the battle in the heavenlies for their souls and that they have the ability to be able to choose good from evil. It is time to make a quality decision that you are going to believe God and what He said about you once and for all. It is time to let the Holy Spirit program you to greatness and to peace.

James 1:8 says a double minded man is unstable in all his ways. You have one foot over here, one foot over there. One day you are in the kingdom of Satan, the next day in the kingdom of God. You are split right down the middle. I drew a picture one time of a man split right down the middle. One side of him was white; the other side of him was shaded gray and black.

There were words printed on the white side that were the opposite of the words printed on the left side. The left side that was dark said "hate." The right side said "love." The word on the dark said "unforgiveness." The one on the right said "forgiveness." The one on the left hand side said "lust." The other one said "love."

So in this man standing there split down the middle, we saw the picture of mankind, good and evil, and then Christ being there to redeem him. It is a profound statement of what God created and what needs to be redeemed. Your mind needs to be renewed by the Shepherd. Your mind needs to be renewed by the washing of the water of the Word. You need to have your thinking changed. Even when the evil spirit is removed, you still have your own brain to deal with because you have been programmed with the evil doctrine of devils that came to you from whatever source it came from, either from men, from women, from families, or even from spiritual teachers that taught you a lie.

It's going to take your participation in order to get the Unloving spirit defeated. You are going to have to take a firm stand to take your life back. This one is not going to go down without a fight because it controls you in every aspect of your life. It separates you from the love of God, separates you from loving yourself, and separates you from loving others. It has to be put under your feet. You are going to have to stand by faith no matter what it is screaming in your mind and say,

"I am the righteousness of God through Christ Jesus by faith, and I am being led by the Spirit of God. I am not an accident, and I am here at the express permission of God. According to Psalm 139 I stand here, God, and accept who I am once and for all before You, Amen."

Every lying thought that comes against you in that declaration of your heart, you have to put it under your feet whether you feel like it or not.

We need to get the eternal picture, we need to get our stinkin' thinkin' renewed and we need to get our minds renewed by the washing of the water of the Word, which is the voice of the great Shepherd. So when you are reading your Scriptures and it tells you something, your mind is being renewed by that Word you are reading, but, in fact, you are following the voice of Jesus, the Shepherd. So when you are obedient to the Word of God, you are following the voice of the Shepherd which is for your safety and your benefit.

The world is filled with many voices. First Corinthians 14:10 says there are many voices in the world, none without significance. Every voice coming has something to say. There are many voices. There are many modalities of spirituality.

The intent behind the scenes and behind every person is either the Spirit of God, bringing the kingdom of God or there are various spirits bringing in the kingdom of Satan to control and to rule your life. There is an agenda, a motivation, an intent, a diabolic plan to control and rule you so that the antichrist spirit can rule you. When the antichrist spirit rules you, the kingdom of our Christ is dethroned in the earth through you and that is the intent.

Everyone is saying something about something. But can you find it in the voice of the great Shepherd? If you can't find it in context, it was not Him speaking. There are so many people so interested in esoteric knowledge these days.

First Corinthians 8:1 says, "Knowledge puffeth up. It's vanity." It is amazing that we are looking for esoteric knowledge and we have not mastered what is in Genesis to Revelation. The Christian church has been here for 2,000 years, and we are not even doing what the early apostles in the early church ever did. We are just barely understanding it, let alone walking in it.

What happened to the days when our shadow would fall on someone and they would be healed? What happened to the day when a letter or a cloth or a handkerchief would be sent out and evil spirits would flee and diseases would be healed? What happened to the days of the apostles in the early church? It did not pass away, we did.

Take this principality of the Unloving spirit and start choking him with the Word of God. Get him by his scrawny neck and hang him right up here and look at him. Colossians says,

> ¹²Giving thanks unto the Father, which hath made us meet to be partakers of the inheritance of the saints in light:
> ¹³Who hath delivered us from the power of darkness, and hath translated *us* into the kingdom of his dear Son:
>
> Colossians 1:12-13

That word "light" means the Word.

> Thy word *is* a lamp unto my feet, and a light unto my path.
> Psalm 119:105

Let's understand that the word "light" in Scripture is the written Word of God. The Word of God is light.

We are looking at holding every thought in captivity. It is impossible to be free of an Unloving spirit if you do not follow Christ. It is an antichrist spirit that accuses you because it defies the Word of God concerning you and your acceptance of God. John says this about the Word, which is Jesus,

> ¹In the beginning was the Word, and the Word was with God, and the Word was God.
> ²The same was in the beginning with God.
> ³All things were made by him; and without him was not any thing made that was made.
> ⁴In him was life; and the life was the light of men.
> ⁵And the light shineth in darkness; and the darkness comprehended it not.
> John 1:1-5

BECOME ONE WITH TRUTH

John 1 is talking about the person of God the Word that manifested Himself in the flesh as Jesus Christ. The people did not understand He was the Word standing before them. The Law was standing before them. The Word was standing before them; they touched Him, they handled Him, they saw Him and they did not comprehend that the Word had

115

become incarnate and stood looking at them. The very Word that spoke them into existence was standing, looking at them and they did not comprehend the Word of God. The Word is a person. It is not the philosophy of men. Men have philosophies, but the Word is the philosophy incarnate, the very essence of everything.

There was a man sent from God named John who came for a witness, to bear witness.

> ⁶There was a man sent from God, whose name *was* John.
> ⁷The same came for a witness, to bear witness of the Light, that all *men* through him might believe.　　　John 1:6-7

That word "Light" is capitalized because it is a personal pronoun. The light in one scripture is little "l" and all of a sudden we have it as capital "L." That Light that shineth is equal to a person. The Word of God is called a person; He is called God Himself that was in the beginning with God in the eternal Godhead. In verse 7, to bear witness of the Light that all men through Him might believe. John was not that Light, as capital "L," but was sent to bear witness of that Light, capital "L." That was the true Light, capital "L," the true person Light, which lighteth. Now here is the little "l." The person who is light, which is the word lighteth, now we have little "l," lighteth every man that cometh into the world. It means the Word of God, who is a person, but is a written form also, when that is perceived, and what He has said is understood and comes into you, it lights you on the inside with truth. You become one not only with the philosophy of truth, you become one with the person of truth.

That is how you can be in Christ and that is how you can be in the Father, because Jesus is the Word of the Father and when you are in the truth of God's Word, you are in the Father because you are one with truth. When you are one

116

with truth, you are one with the person who is the truth. This is becoming one with God. It does not make you a god, but makes you part of the very essence of God and His nature. You will not then listen to lies. When you get hold of the Word of God and believe it, you will not listen to lies.

An Unloving spirit is a lie. When you do not love yourself, you are listening to a lie. When someone puts you down and does not love you, does not care for you, does not nurture you and you believe them, then you are listening to a lie of the devil. They become an oracle of truth concerning you, not from God, but from the devil who is the thief and the hireling that has come to kill you and to steal from you and destroy you.

If you review your life, if you have listened to the voice of the Unloving spirit, then you are killed, you are destroyed, you are devastated, and you know it because that is the fruit of it. The fruit of an Unloving spirit is that you are killed, you have been stolen from, and you are destroyed.

You become a non-person and that is due to an antichrist spirit because the Word of God says you are the apple of His eye. If you can believe this today, God will set you free from that foul spirit. If you do not believe it, then you are following a false shepherd and he is not going to protect you, he is going to destroy you.

"There was a true Light that lighteth every man who cometh into the world. He was in the world and the world was made by Him (that means Jesus is the Creator of all mankind) and the world (or mankind) knew Him not. He came unto His own (that would be the Jews, the Old Testament church) and His own received Him not. But as many as received Him to them gave He power to become the sons of God."

117

⁸He was not that Light, but *was sent* to bear witness of that Light.

⁹*That* was the true Light, which lighteth every man that cometh into the world.

¹⁰He was in the world, and the world was made by him, and the world knew him not.

¹¹He came unto his own, and his own received him not.

¹²But as many as received him, to them gave he power to become the sons of God, *even* to them that believe on his name: John 1:8-12

Have you received Christ? If you have received Christ, it is impossible for you to hate yourself. It is impossible unless you call Him a liar while you are in Him. You are telling Him that you are not loved and you are listening to that lie.

John and Matthew say,

¹²But as many as received him, to them gave he power to become the sons of God, *even* to them that believe on his name:

¹³Which were born, not of blood, nor of the will of the flesh, nor of the will of man, but of God.

¹⁴And the Word was made flesh, and dwelt among us, (and we beheld his glory, the glory as of the only begotten of the Father,) full of grace and truth.   John 1:12-14

¹³And leaving Nazareth, he came and dwelt in Capernaum, which is upon the sea coast, in the borders of Zabulon and Nephthalim:

¹⁴That it might be fulfilled which was spoken by Esaias the prophet, saying,

¹⁵The land of Zabulon, and the land of Nephthalim, *by* the way of the sea, beyond Jordan, Galilee of the Gentiles;

¹⁶The people which sat in darkness saw great light; and to them which sat in the region and shadow of death light is sprung up.

¹⁷From that time Jesus began to preach, and to say, Repent: for the kingdom of heaven is at hand.   Matthew 4:13-17

The big "L" showed up to bring that light; it is a little "l" in this verse. They were sitting in darkness. They were separated from the truth of God's Word. He was the living Light, the living Word of God, walking into their presence to show them God's love for them. "From that time on, Jesus began to preach and say, 'Repent for the kingdom of heaven is at hand.' "

The kingdom of heaven is the rulership of creation by Jesus Christ specifically on this planet, but who lives on the planet? You do. You live on the planet and all of your seed and all of your prosperity. The kingdom of heaven is at hand, repent. What do you need to repent for? Allowing, believing and listening to a lie. You have been programmed by your ancestry, you have been programmed by your mother and your father, your grandparents and even husbands and wives to be unloved; and you have believed.

You have made it part of your life because of the circumstances of your life, but doing so is the work of an antichrist spirit because God has redeemed you. You have listened to His call, you have accepted the Word in your life, and you have accepted your sonship and your daughtership of the living God. No longer are you bastards. You are adopted into the family of God whereby you can cry out, "Abba, Father." What does that word "bastard" mean? It means "spiritually separated from your Father." A birth by a father that is not the true Father. Birthed, but you are not bastards, you are children of God!

Isaiah says,

> [1]Nevertheless the dimness *shall* not *be* such as *was* in her vexation, when at the first he lightly afflicted the land of Zebulun and the land of Naphtali, and afterward did more grievously afflict *her by* the way of the sea, beyond Jordan, in Galilee of the nations.
> [2]The people who walked in darkness have seen a great light: they that dwell in the land of the shadow of death, upon them hath the light shined.　　　Isaiah 9:1-2

You are walking in the valley of the shadow of death because an unclean, Unloving spirit is death to you; it is death to your spirit. It is a crusher to your human spirit that separates you from the love of God, separates you from who you are in creation and separates you from others. Someone has to get spiritual here. Do you have ears to hear?

In Revelation 2 and 3, when the Lord spoke to the seven churches, He said this: "He that hath an ear, let him hear what the Spirit is saying to the seven churches. He that hath an ear, let him hear..." If that you have an ear now, hear what the Spirit of God is saying to your heart.

You are either going to reject this or you are going to believe it. If you do not believe the Word of God coming to you, you are listening to the devil, and you have just listened to a lie. I do not care what that replay button is doing from the past in your generation. I do not care what mommy or daddy may have said to you yesterday, I do not care what they told you five minutes ago, it's a lie. If they do not love you and accept you, they have an antichrist spirit, and they are of the devil to your life. To the degree that we do not follow the voice of the great Shepherd and that we follow the voice of the hireling and the false shepherd, we are of the spirit of the hireling and the false shepherd; we are of the devil. The truth of God is not in us.

Everything that is screaming on the inside of you right now, you need to tell it to go because it is an antichrist spirit from the devil and wants to kill you, steal from you and destroy you. What are you going to do about that? Whose report will you believe? Whose voice are you following? The voices from within? Are you following truth or are you following a lie? You need to make up your mind that you are not going to listen to lies anymore. Be a man or woman of God and ask God to show you the part of your life that is not lined up with the Word.

Do you remember what Peter said when Jesus confronted him? Jesus came to Peter and said, "I want to wash your feet." Peter said, "No way, You are not going to wash my feet, You are the Lord, and I am just no one, I am rejected, I am hot-tempered, and I am always getting in trouble. I should be washing Your feet, Lord." Jesus said, "If you do not let Me wash your feet, you have no part in Me."

Peter got the message really clear from the great Shepherd. He said, Lord, wash me all over. Get the bucket and pour it from the top. Peter said that because he did not want to be separated from the Word and the Light. When the Lord comes to wash my little stinky feet, I say, Lord, wash me all over, get out the Q-tips, get out the washcloths, get out the high-powered pressure hoses, get out those little lights that the doctor sticks in your nose and your ear, and look in there. If there be any wicked thing in me, You get it out, Lord, because I am only going to follow Your voice. Get those critters out. The Bible says this, in the last days there are those who will call evil good and good evil.

> **Woe unto them that call evil good, and good evil; that put darkness for light, and light for darkness; that put bitter for sweet, and sweet for bitter!** Isaiah 5:20

If you go into integration and fusion, they will tell you that an Unloving spirit is just one of your archetypes and you just need to come to grips with it and integrate it into your personality so you can have a better life. Sorry, but that's unscriptural. Your mind is being renewed by the washing of the water of the Word, not by being integrated with that garbage. Number one, you need to get the evil spirit out. Number two, you need to get your mind straightened out to believe the Word of God. Amen?

Colossians says,

> ¹²Giving thanks unto the Father, which hath made us meet to be partakers of the inheritance of the saints in light:
> ¹³Who hath delivered us from the power of darkness, and hath translated *us* into the kingdom of his dear Son:
> ¹⁴In whom we have redemption through his blood, *even* the forgiveness of sins:
> ¹⁵Who is the image of the invisible God, the firstborn of every creature:
> ¹⁶For by him were all things created, that are in heaven, and that are in earth, visible and invisible, whether they be thrones, or dominions, or principalities, or powers: all things were created by him, and for him:
> ¹⁷And he is before all things, and by him all things consist.
> ¹⁸And he is the head of the body, the church: who is the beginning, the firstborn from the dead; that in all things he might have the preeminence.
> ¹⁹For it pleased the Father that in him should all fulness dwell;
> ²⁰And, having made peace through the blood of his cross, by him to reconcile all things unto himself; by him, I say, whether they be things in earth, or things in heaven.
> ²¹And you, that were sometime alienated and enemies in your mind by wicked works, yet now hath he reconciled
> ²²In the body of his flesh through death, to present you holy and unblameable and unreproveable in his sight:
> ²³If ye continue in the faith grounded and settled, and be not moved away from the hope of the gospel, which ye have heard, and which was preached to every creature which is under heaven; whereof I Paul am made a minister;
>
> Colossians 1:12-23

"For it pleased the Father that in Him (the Son) shall all fullness dwell. Having made peace through the blood of His cross by Him to reconcile all things unto Himself by Him I say whether they be in earth or things in heaven. You that were sometimes alienated (separated) and enemies in your mind."

You can be an enemy in your own mind, and your own mind can be your enemy. Did you ever have a battle with

122

yourself mentally? Have you ever put yourself down intellectually? Have you ever put yourself down mentally with words and pictures? That is being alienated from yourself. That is being in opposition to yourself. That is having a battle with yourself. Do you know what is so funny? When someone else victimizes you, then you end up having a battle with yourself over it. Someone else had the problem, you took it into yourself, and now you are fighting yourself. You can't love yourself if you are putting yourself down. Here you put yourself down, and the Spirit of God comes and says, "Yeah but, you are the apple of My eye." You say, "Go away Holy Spirit, I am putting myself down."

You that were sometimes alienated and enemies in your mind by wicked works, yet now hath He reconciled in the body of His flesh through death to present you holy and... What is self-accusation going to do now? What is self-rejection going to do? What is self-hatred going to do? What is an Unloving spirit going to do? How can you allow the antichrist spirit of unloveliness to put you down when the Father just said through the Word, through Christ, you are unblameable.

"To present you holy, and unblameable and unreproveable in His sight if..." There is now a condition. "If ye continue in the faith grounded and settled and be not moved away from the hope of the gospel which you have heard and which was preached to every creature which is under heaven, wherein I Paul am made a minister."

Colossians says,

> 4And this I say, lest any man should beguile you with enticing words.
> 5For though I be absent in the flesh, yet am I with you in the spirit, joying and beholding your order, and the steadfastness of your faith in Christ.
> 6As ye have therefore received Christ Jesus the Lord, *so* walk ye in him: Colossians 2:4-6

123

What is meant by walking in Christ? Believe what He said and do it! Accept what He said! You are loved of God! Believe it and walk in it!

What do you do when the devil comes to accuse you and remind you of those unrenewed parts of your life that you are working on? The worst thing you can do is to start listening to those voices in your head. What happens when the insurance agent shows up at your door and he wants to sell you insurance? Slam, don't need any, bam! Right? You go down here to Wal-Mart, and someone is selling something on the sidewalk. You say, "No I don't need any today," and keep on moving. Or maybe you give them something or buy something out of guilt. Both!

Why do you allow your enemy to come into your minds and say, "I have some dastardly deeds to discuss with you today concerning your life." You say, "Oh, what are they? Give me the list. Only half of them are true, oh me, oh my."

The devil came to me one day in his kingdom in that dimension, and I listened to it for a few weeks. The Bible says,

> ...When the enemy shall come in like a flood, the Spirit of the LORD shall lift up a standard against him.   Isaiah 59:19

You need to let the Holy Spirit have access to your life. When you can't handle it, He will, if you will let Him. But you have to yield and open the door and say, "Holy Spirit, will you please deal with this?" He will.

I told this thing that was chewing my ears off, spouting those voices and images, "Hey you! If I have a problem, it is none of your business because you are not my Father. I have a Father in heaven, and if I have a spiritual problem, it is His problem not yours, so get lost."

I said, "Father, can we start talking about this? I need your help, and this is true, the enemy did come and tell me this is an area in which he has access to my life. This is not a false accusation, and I feel convicted about this. You are my Father and You said You love me, and if I confess my sins then You are faithful and just to forgive me of my sins. Father, I really need Your help to work in this area of my life." Instantly I came under the protection of the Father. When you listen to those voices, you come under the protection of Satan. He comes to kill, steal, and destroy. Whose report shall you believe? I shall believe the report of the Lord.

I am establishing the Word of God in your hearts by teaching you. I am bringing Jesus the Word right into your spirit. "As you have been taught abounding therein with thanksgiving."

Glory to God, I thank you God! I am getting my spirit filled with Jesus the Word. Hallelujah, I just thank you God! That is thanksgiving.

If someone saved you from drowning you would say, "Oh I can't believe you did it. You jumped in the water and got all wet. Are you okay? You saved my life!?" But Jesus saves our life and we go, "Alright, thanks Lord. I will call You sometime when I need You, when I am drowning again. What is Your number again, Lord?"

Colossians says,

> **Beware lest any man spoil you through philosophy and vain deceit, after the tradition of men, after the rudiments of the world, and not after Christ.** Colossians 2:8

To win this battle between your ears, be prepared to be reprogrammed by the mind of Christ versus the mind of Satan. What is meant by your mind being renewed by the washing of the water of the Word? Your thoughts can be changed, and you can hold every thought in captivity. Subject those old memes to new ones that make more sense representing the mind of Christ.

Colossians says,

> And have put on the new *man,* which is renewed in knowledge after the image of him that created him:
>
> Colossians 3:10

First Corinthians says,

> For who hath known the mind of the Lord, that he may instruct him? But we have the mind of Christ.
>
> 1 Corinthians 2:16

When you have the mind of Christ, you have the Word of God within your spirit. Your mind being renewed by the Word of God means now your thinking at the spiritual level and the mind level have become one.

Let your spirit and mind become one.

Your thinking in the spirit dimension and in the physical dimension are now one. No longer are you double minded. You can tuck scripture away in your heart, but your mind may pitch a fit and cause you to do something else. You disobey God first in the mind, not in the spirit. When you disobey God in the mind realm, it becomes a spiritual defect to you because your spirit is now being hardened with a lie, which is antichrist. The Word of God is truth, it is light, and everything that is contradictory to it must be cast down because it is detrimental to your health, and the mind of Christ.

Colossians 2:8 says, "Beware lest any man spoil you."

You are changing your thinking. If your thinking does not match the Word, you have to change it. Do you want to believe a lie? Then why do you? "Beware lest any man spoil
126

you through philosophy." Philosophy, most of it, is the doctrine of devils. It is mankind saying what mankind is all about, and has nothing to do with what God said. Philosophy is man's attempt to become an oracle for himself. If philosophy does not match what the Word of God has said, then what do you do with it? Do you believe it or do you cast it down? You cast it down. Is that changing your thinking? Is that your mind being renewed?

Maybe the philosophy of your home was that you were a stinking piece of garbage that should never have been born. Now are you going to believe that or are you going to cast it down? You used to believe it. Now you cast it down because the Word of God has come and said you are the righteousness of God through Christ Jesus, you are the apple of His eye, you are engraved in the palms of His hands, you are the bride of Christ, you are kings and priests forever, you are sons and daughters of God.

That is what the Word says and God loves you, and let every man be a liar who says otherwise. Now whose report are you going to believe? My mind has been renewed concerning my identity. I am not a victim anymore. I am a slave to Jesus Christ and my slavery to Him is my freedom because He is the Creator, and He is the Word. He is total freedom. Whoever the Son makes free is free indeed.

I refuse to be a slave to the beggarly elements of the world anymore, on any count, under any authority, by any man, devil or otherwise angel. The Word of God is my standard; what it says about me and you, past, present and future is the only thing I am going to believe, and let every other voice that speaks be cast down as a liar spirit of destruction. You are going to have to come to this if you are going to be free.

It is not what your mommy and daddy said about you or did to you; it is what God has said about you, and you have to believe it. Whenever my kids get on the wrong side of the fence, I look at them straight in the eye and say, "Are you a son of Satan or a son of God? I demand an answer." They look at me and say, "A son of God, Daddy." "Then act like it." That is instilling the mind of Christ into them that they are sons of God by faith in the making. Hallelujah.

"Beware lest any man spoil you through philosophy and vain deceit after the traditions of men, after the rudiments of the world and not after Christ. For in Him (that is Christ) dwelleth all the fullness of the Godhead bodily. You are complete in Him which is the head of all principality and power."

> For in him dwelleth all the fulness of the Godhead bodily. And ye are complete in him, which is the head of all principality and power: Colossians 2:9-10

So all those Unloving, unclean spirits that are within you get to answer to the Lord. If you are complete in the Lord, who is the head of you as well as all principalities and powers, those principalities and powers have to bow their knee to the Word of God also. That is why we can cast them out in His name.

They have to obey because He is the head of all things visible and invisible, whether they be principalities or powers or spiritual wickedness in high places, obedient and disobedient spirits, devils and angels and created beings, man included. All are under the authority of God the Word.

It pleased the Father to put all things under His authority. That is why we call Jesus Lord. In Him we have light and we have freedom and we have been restored to what God created us to be. Bless God, Amen and Amen, so be it.

128

THE BATTLE

Are you ready to defeat this principality? Do you want to put them under your feet? Are you ready to take your life back and be propelled into heavenly places where you are seated with Christ Jesus far above all principalities and powers? Get back on your throne and take dominion. Who do you start to rule? Principalities and powers. Just tell them what to do in the name of Jesus. Say,

"You unclean spirit, I am a daughter of the most high God. In the name of Jesus Christ of Nazareth who is the Word of God, you get out of my life! You stop tormenting me, you are a lying spirit and I refuse to listen to you anymore."

If you will take that attack, the devil will be defeated in your life and God will honor you because that is His Word and that is His will.

**When you line up with the Word of God
and the will of God,
all of heaven is moved on your behalf.**

You need to get a life and get eternal in Christ because He is the head of all principality and power. So when the Unloving spirit comes along and says, "I don't think you are very important," you say, "But the Lord says I am the apple of His eye." "No you're not, that is a lie." "No, you are a liar, you are an antichrist spirit, get out of my life." Are you ready to fight that kind of war? Are you ready to take your life back? Are you ready to believe that you are special?

Second Corinthians says,

³**For though we walk in the flesh, we do not war after the flesh:**
⁴**(For the weapons of our warfare *are* not carnal, but mighty through God to the pulling down of strong holds;)**

⁵Casting down imaginations, and every high thing that exalteth itself against the knowledge of God, and bringing into captivity every thought to the obedience of Christ;

⁶And having in a readiness to revenge all disobedience, when your obedience is fulfilled.   2 Corinthians 10:3-6

Give your enemy fair warning: we are going to slash him to pieces. This is the fulcrum point of your freedom. If you can't defeat the Unloving spirit, everything else will have a heyday in your life. Would you like to be in a battle all of your life, or would you just like to get on with your life? You are going to have to stop listening to this big lie that you have been programmed with from childhood, saying you are not accepted, you are not here, or that you do not belong here.

Any man, woman or child that would tell you so is a liar. This is the battle for your life. If your life is not changed forever, you have wasted your time. These unclean spirits have destroyed you all your life. A double minded man is unstable in all his ways.

A double minded man *is* unstable in all his ways.
James 1:8

You have to be able to start seeing yourself as God saw you when He created you from the foundation of the world, and you have to start conforming to the image of the Word concerning that. You do not have any option, because if you go any other way, you are being led by an antichrist spirit. Romans 8:14 says, "For as many as are led by the Spirit of God are the sons (and daughters) of God." For as many as are not led by the Spirit of God are led by the antichrist spirit of the devil and are having difficulty becoming the sons and daughters of God. The more you listen to the lies of men and doctrines of devils through men, beginning in your family traditions, in your family trees going back 50 generations into your own mother and father, and uncles and aunts, and grandparents, and husbands and wives, and in your own personal life, the more you have listened to that garbage of abuse and have taken it into your life, to that degree Satan rules you. That is the foundation of your thoughts. **Who will you believe?**

You are important to God. You are important to Jesus. You are important to the Holy Ghost. In war, they used to say, "Give no quarter to the enemy." That means, "Do not give place to the devil or the enemy; do not budge an inch."

Ephesians 6:13 says, "When having done all, to stand." What is the worst thing that can happen to you? You die and go to heaven, so what is your problem? Fear of death, Fear of dying, Fear of man, Fear of failure, Fear of Fear. You will never defeat Fear if you do not defeat this Unloving spirit.

You will never defeat Fear if you do not accept yourself in God through Jesus Christ; you will never defeat it because you do not have the power. The Holy Spirit is not going to honor Fear; He is only going to honor faith. That is why Jesus said, "According to your faith, so be it unto you," in Matthew 9:29.

Are you going to take charge of your life? Are you going to take your life back? Then do it. "Let God be true and every man a liar." If you want to cross those devils that are lying through man, what do you have going for you?

Discernment! Discernment gives you the ability to deal with it, not take it into yourself. Do not take the words of others into yourself because Satan is trying to program you into abuse and destruction with an antichrist spirit that will steal your identity in Christ from the foundation of the world. You are going to have to say, "I am not going there." You can do that and never have to be delivered of one evil spirit. You can have the whole congregation of them on the inside of you, and you can defeat them just by your belief in God and His Word and who you are in Him.

How many thoughts do you have a day that you do not follow through on? In a given day, awake or asleep, you have at least 100 thoughts that come from somewhere that you do not act on, that you cast down. Choose this day what you shall have, blessings or cursings, life or death.

> I call heaven and earth to record this day against you, *that* I have set before you life and death, blessing and cursing: therefore choose life, that both thou and thy seed may live:
>
> Deuteronomy 30:19

The world is programmed by Satan for death, hell and destruction. You can preach all the peace you want, but until mankind gets right with God, there is no peace. There never has been, and there never will be until the Prince of Peace comes to deal with it. You are going to come back with Him and help Him deal with it. How can you help subdue the enemies of Christ in the millennium if you are not even willing to do it now? Be not weary in well doing. Second Corinthians says,

> When I was a child, I spake as a child, I understood as a child, I thought as a child: but when I became a man, I put away childish things. For now we see through a glass, darkly; but then face to face: now I know in part; but then shall I know even as also I am known.   1 Corinthians 13:11-12

That is a tremendous statement about who you will be in the future of eternity. You will be known as you are known. Who you are now is who you are going to be then. It is time to change, because I do not want to be known totally in the future as I am known today.

Proverbs 22:15 says that evil (foolishness) is bound up in the heart of a child.

Children are so petty. At times they are so naïve and so wonderful in their ability to love each other and to have fellowship. At other times... Wait a minute. We were children at one time. Where did we learn all this evil? Most of it began in our childhood. Then we became adults, and we ended up living it even further.

There are many women who had abusive fathers, and when they married, their husband was just like their father. Or perhaps a man's mother abused him emotionally and did not care for him, then the man married and he would have a wife just like his cold fish mother. Many people marry what they hated the most. To explain spiritual dynamics in the inherited spiritual curse, there are forces within you that will draw you to the like thing. Like begets like.

There are forces within you that will hook up with the same type of forces in others to produce the same type of devastation, so you need to have your eyes wide open. Have your eyes wide open in any relationship you have which could lead to of marriage. You two had better sit down and talk about your childhood, your life, your ancestral line and be very honest with each other because what you do not deal with up front will surface in your marriage, and it won't go away. Evil spirits must manifest, and they will manifest.

I have coined a ministry term in teaching called "timed release." As God has a plan for your life, so does the devil. As God plans to bring you progressively to a place of your maturity as a son or daughter of God, I believe the devil has a plan to take you in just the opposite direction and destroy you and leave you devastated and embittered in old age. I believe the devil's plan is that the desolation of your childhood will be the desolation of your adulthood and will be the desolation of your golden years. That needs to change somewhere. If you were abused as a child, then you need to put away childish things. It is time for you to be a mature man or woman of God, free from abuse. "When I was a child, I thought as a child." I do not have to act out the desolation of my generations.

I do not have to do to my children what was done to me. I do not have to do anything. I am a freewill agent, born again, filled with the Spirit of God, having the Word of God. I am a new creature in Christ Jesus. I am not what I was. I am not what I shall be. I am being changed from glory to glory, and I love every moment of it. That old thing is passed away. Behold all things are become new, and I have my eyes on eternity. I have my eyes on what God has said about me as His child, and I am going there. "Let God be true and every man a liar."

You do not have to live the desolation of your ancestry or your personal life any longer.

James says, "If any of you lack wisdom, let him ask of God that giveth to all men liberally and upbraideth not and it shall be given him. But let him ask in faith, nothing wavering. For he that wavereth is like a wave of the sea driven with the wind and tossed, but let not that man think that he shall receive anything of the Lord. A double minded man is unstable in all his ways."

> [5]If any of you lack wisdom, let him ask of God, that giveth to all *men* liberally, and upbraideth not; and it shall be given him.
> [6]But let him ask in faith, nothing wavering. For he that wavereth is like a wave of the sea driven with the wind and tossed.
> [7]For let not that man think that he shall receive any thing of the Lord.
> [8]A double minded man *is* unstable in all his ways.
> James 1:5-8

134

That scripture sets the foundation for all fragmentation of the human spirit and human personality. It says "tossed to and fro." All insanity, manic depression, paranoid schizophrenia, psychotics, split personality, type A personality and multiple personality disorder are rooted in double mindedness.

All of it is a result of personal, family and historical abuse and Rejection, abuse and control of the human spirit and soul, spiritually and emotionally, by the devil so that the he can produce seed after himself. God created you to be His seed, the seed of righteousness in the earth.

The devil wants this earth to be inhabited using God's seed, taking them to be his children and then teaching them his dastardly deeds so that they can be the seed of his spiritual genetics in the earth, and so you will be the extension of the evil spiritual dynamics of your mother and father and ancestry, *ad infinitum*, eternally until this planet is destroyed and the purposes of God are overthrown.

That is the master plan of Satan. So where do you fit into it? As children who have no understanding or as mature, spiritual adults who have understanding? What are you going to do about it? The odds are against you doing anything about it for anyone else, so what's left? You have to do it for yourself.

Turn, O backsliding children, saith the Lord; for I am married unto you: and I will take you one of a city, and two of a family, and I will bring you to Zion: Jeremiah 3:14

God takes two of a family and one of a city. He brings them to Himself in spite of the master plan of Satan to destroy mankind spiritually. Satan wants to bring death, hell and destruction and to kill, steal and destroy.

When God saved you He said, "That is enough." Now what are you going to do to respond to that? Are you going to walk in the devastation of your ancestry or walk in the provision of the God who saved you?

You have two areas of your existence that need attention. This antichrist spirit produces disobedience to God in the area of accepting who you are in Christ and not accepting and loving yourself; there is the kingdom of Self, self-introspection, Self-Pity, inversion and looking in. That whole kingdom is reinforced on two dimensions: your human spirit and your human soul or your intellect.

READ THE BIBLE

If you are going to win this battle; it is going to take more than deliverance. It is going to take more than casting the evil spirit out that is Unloving, because when you have done that, you still have yourself to deal with. That is why deliverance by itself sometimes fails. That would violate the scripture that says your mind is renewed by the washing of the water of the Word. That would violate the scripture in 2 Corinthians 10:5 that says we are to hold every thought in captivity, casting down imaginations and everything that would exalt itself against the knowledge of God, which is the Word of God. That is why you need to read your Bible whether you feel like it or not.

When I read my Bible, it is just as if God sat down, took me by the hand and said, "I want to talk to you, sir." I read my Bible just that way. Every story that is in there about evil and good, I put my name right in it. When Peter betrayed Christ, I did that. When Eve listened to the devil and partook of that fruit of the tree of knowledge of good and evil, I learned from that.

When Jonah would not go to Nineveh and ended up in a whale of a mess, I learned from that. When I saw evil being done even by God's people in the Bible, except by the grace of God, so there go I. It might as well have just been me, because I am a member of the human race. Every word in Scripture, every theme, every concept, every jot, every tittle, every word of instruction — I hang on every word. If you want to sit at the feet of the Master, read what He said.

There are so many people chasing gurus and sitting at the feet of descended masters, hanging on every word. Why can't we hang on the Word of the living God and not the imposter who is trying to imitate Him? I think there is a spirit in the world that puts us to sleep spiritually.

God's people are the laziest, most selfish individuals because we have been given such a great inheritance, and we consider it like we are having a bowl of pottage because we are hungry. In the world today, the church is not really acting very excited about God and the One who created them, the One who saved them and the One who redeemed them.

Concerning the church at Laodicea in Revelation 3, Jesus said, "I wish you were hot. I wish you were cold. But because you are lukewarm, I am going to spew you out of My mouth." It is not time to be lukewarm. It is not time to be cold. It is time to be hot concerning God and your life. It is time for you to take the instruction that you are getting from the throne room of God right now and the Word of God that is amplified right here, apply it to your life and get on with it! Dress up in who God created you to be! Put off the spirit of heaviness. Put on the garment of praise!

When you read about the armor in Ephesians, you are to dress up in it. Your feet are to be shod with the preparation of the gospel of peace, your loins girt about with truth. You

137

put on the breastplate of righteousness, the helmet of salvation, the sword of the Spirit. What is flashing in front of your principalities and powers as you are reading this? The sword of the Spirit, which is the Word of God.

Hebrews says,

> [12]For the word of God *is* quick, and powerful, and sharper than any twoedged sword, piercing even to the dividing asunder of soul and spirit, and of the joints and marrow, and *is* a discerner of the thoughts and intents of the heart.
> [13]Neither is there any creature that is not manifest in his sight: but all things *are* naked and opened unto the eyes of him with whom we have to do.   Hebrews 4:12-13

If you apply this to your life, the devil will be defeated. You will be a better person for it, and God will get the glory. You say, "Well I might not know who I am, because you are stripping so much off of me. I will not exist anymore. I am in confusion. I am in Fear. Who am I?"

That is probably the most sane question you ever asked in your life: who am I? A specific child. A specific person. A specific individual. A specific part of creation that is uniquely necessary and needed for eternity. You are uniquely created, uniquely crafted, uniquely part of the corporate body of Christ for eternity, as the mystical bride of Christ.

Every one of you is uniquely different and uniquely necessary. Each of you brings a different dimension of God's glory and His testimony of creation! You have to see yourself that way! This unclean spirit, this antichrist spirit, this type of disobedience to God, this Unloving spirit, this Self-Pity, this kingdom of Self and self-preservation have to go because they are built on Satan's foundation and have been reinforced in your life from the generations.

138

The Bible says that if an evil spirit is cast out of you, and you are not filled up, it is going to come back and find out if your house is filled or empty. If it finds your house empty of truth, knowledge, power, glory and all that you have been taught, and if there is no teaching there, no resolve there, if there is no execution of your will there, if there is no dedication to who you are in Christ there, that spirit is going to come right back in and bring seven more much worse than itself.

The latter state of your case will be much worse than the former state. That is why deliverance ministries can be very dangerous. You are going to have to execute your sovereignty because the antichrist spirit in your generations, in your family, has taken away your sovereignty.

You have always been under the thumb of someone, usually in victimization. That is a type of control that is witchcraft control. Witchcraft is always rooted in hatred of God, an antichrist mentality and Fear. Fear is so strong because the devil's greatest spiritual problem is Fear.

The being that is more afraid than you can imagine is Lucifer now fallen, known as Satan. He has more Fear than any lower, lesser devil you can imagine. Fear is strong in the earth because that is his nature. He is rejected of God. He is rejected of men. He is rejected of two-thirds of all angels. He is judged, and the Bible says that he even knows he is.

"The devil, knowing his time is short, goes about like a roaring lion, seeking whom he may devour." He says he is going to get you today and you say, "No way, I am filled up." What do you need to do with the devil and his kingdom? Put up a sign up that says, "Unloving spirit, No Vacancy." You can't defeat an Unloving spirit unless you totally put him in submission to the Word as to who you are in creation. Whether you ever arrive spiritually or not, that is between you and God.

I accept you as an equal, not as a second-rate, bastard child of the devil. I consider you equal in the Father through Jesus Christ, with no one having supremacy over another. You are necessary to the completeness of the body, and I accept you as an equal. Would you please receive? Thank you! I do not judge people on the basis of success or failure, wealth or poverty, tall or short, looks or no looks, ups or downs.

I judge people only by the inner man and God's ordination of them from the foundation of the world. I make no distinction between men and women on the basis of anything. I love the weak as well as the strong; I love you all equally, and I have no favorites. That is how the Lord meets you, and if I am going to be an extension of the Lord, I have to meet you right where you are.

I do not judge you after your rages, I do not judge you after your battles, nor do I judge you after your failures. I judge you after God's heart for you from the foundation of the world, and my job is to teach you, to lead you as a shepherd and to execute the kingdom of God and the kingdom of heaven in your hearts, Amen.

Someone said the other day, "Pastor, when you preach, you preach like you are preaching to thousands." I will preach to you one-on-one just as firmly as if I had 10,000 people in a large auditorium. I am just as intense. I will just flash that sword and come right along beside you. Whether it is one person or 10,000, what difference does it make? David learned that lesson, although he learned it the hard way when he numbered Israel. Second Samuel 24:10 says that Satan tempted David to number Israel because David wanted to be ruling over a kingdom that was based on numbers, not based on the call of God in his life.

I laugh when people say, "Well, how big is your church, Pastor?" I say, "In which state?" They have this mentality that if you do not have a large congregation attending in one place you do not have any value for God. Matthew 18:13 says there is greater value for that shepherd that leaves the 99 safe in the fold and goes over the cliff for the one. There is greater rejoicing in heaven for the one that is saved than the 99 that are safe.

What is the greater value? One person. What a paradox! The world teaches that numbers are the test of success. God has taught you from His thinking that one person is the test of success, and that He would have died just for you. In fact, in the flood God made provision, and only eight people listened out of probably about 15 billion.

A New Way of Thinking about Yourself

So in order to defeat these principalities, you have to be able to start seeing yourself on two levels: how you think in your spirit and how you think in your mind. Psychology has taught compartments of the soul, called the conscious and the subconscious. So even in the teaching of Carl Jung and Jungian psychology today, it is taught that you think on two dimensions. The Word of God has taught that you think on two dimensions too, but it is not called the subconscious; it is called the spirit. I consider the subconscious of man a heresy of Scripture.

I consider it a doctrine of devils. The Bible teaches that we are a spirit, we have a soul, and we live in the body. What psychology calls the subconscious of man, the Bible calls the spirit of man. Psychology denies the spirit of man and creates a dualistic compartment of the soul. The spirit is

141

never mentioned. New Age journals consider the spirit and soul to be one. I even saw a Christian article the other day that called the soul the spirit. That is unscriptural and that is error.

The Bible teaches the triuneness of man. First Thessalonians 5:23 says, may the God of peace sanctify you wholly, w-h-o-l-l-y. This is not holy, this is w-h-o-l-l-y.

Who is the God of peace? Jesus is called the Prince of Peace. That is why you run to Him and run to the Father through Him. Then this Unloving spirit can be gone because you have your completeness of being and your acceptance in who you are. May the God of peace sanctify you wholly in spirit, soul and body.

Let's go to Hebrews 4, because I want to help you understand this battle.

Many of you may be delivered of the spirits involved that have produced this in your family tree, but you may continue to have a battle because your mind remembers. Your brain cells are capable of taking pictures. Your brain is not only capable of producing thoughts, but it can do a panoramic view of pictures. Your mind is capable of projecting pictures and full-length movies of your life in living Technicolor with quadraphonic sound included. All of this is going on inside you.

If you are going to take back your life, you are going to have to do some reconstruction after that spirit is broken and gone. You are going to have to rethink your existence from a human perspective so that your brain and your memes (the units of memory that you have been programmed with from childhood in your generations, to be destroyed and be rejected and be abused) allow room for God to work. You are going to have to allow God, and allow yourself, and people around you to love you. You are going to have to be able to believe in and trust that they will care for you, and that they love you whether you are good or bad today. Trust that they will accept you and love you. Over a period of time, you are going to have to start allowing the Spirit of God to reinforce this in your life, and you will reinforce it in your own life so that you establish new memories: a new way of thinking about yourself.

Now you can't take away your memory; it's part of you forever. Long-term memory is a result of protein synthesis, which involves the RNA components of genetics. So in long-term memory, the RNA component of protein synthesis in the brain cells, that image which was taken through word or picture, is impressed and becomes part of you forever. You will remember the abuse done to you or something from the past, but we have found in ministry that when God heals you, you have the memory, but the spirit is gone. Your mind has been renewed, and you are able to walk through it; you have the memory, but the pain is gone. You think about it in your head, but you feel it down here in your abdomen. If you are thinking about anything up here in your head, and you are feeling it down here in your gut, there is a spirit in there giving you the feeling, because that is where your spirit man resides. If you are able to think about that person, that situation, that circumstance, that hurt, that torment which corresponds to thought up here and the feeling down there, and the feeling down there is gone, then what you have left is just the thought without the feeling. That is evidence that the evil spirit is gone.

All evil spirits manifest through the spirit of man, and then gain access to the body and soul over a period of time. You can't make an evil spirit physical because it is a spirit according to Scripture. It is in a different dimension than the physical world. Does the Holy Spirit live in your spirit, your

143

soul or in your body? The Holy Spirit has access to you through your spirit, because He is spirit.

So the Holy Spirit is able to become one with you in the spirit, but because the spirit is attached to the soul, there is a line of communication that occurs. Then He is able to speak to you in such a way that you perceive it through the soul, through impressions and words.

Satan, through his kingdom, approaches you in a similar way, but not entirely the same because Satan cannot come into you directly. Many times he uses a medium, and that medium can even be you yourself. You open yourself up to his thoughts, to his purposes, or sometimes he'll come to you in the form of another as an oracle of the devil, who will speak doctrines of devils to you.

When you believe that and make it part of your understanding, then that spirituality also becomes part of you. That is how you can be trained in error and heresy, as in false religions. You do not have the truth in you. Most people who fall into cults and false religions and error do not know the Bible, but they have a desire for spiritual things because God created us as a spirit. He created us to have a desire to commune with a spirit, and that Spirit was supposed to be the Godhead.

FREEDOM

You need to have the mind of Christ. Your thinking has to be renewed to the image of the Word and the image of God. Your mind needs to be renewed, and your thinking needs to be changed into *a more excellent way.* When it comes to the Unloving spirit, you must subject all of your thinking that is producing the pain of self-rejection, self-hatred, guilt, all the Unloving spirits of Self-Pity, self-introspection and the kingdom of Self to *a more excellent way.* What would be *a more excellent way*? Feeling accepted, and believing God loves you.

How are you able to get yourself out of the control of your past? How are you able to break away from the abuse patterns of what people have done to you in your past? How are you able to be so renewed that those things do not haunt you, torment you, control you and project into you for the future?

The first thing you do is to see who you are in Christ. Then recognize that what controlled them was controlling others before them. The people who tried to control you with abuse — verbal or spiritual or physical or emotional, were first controlled themselves by someone else. You need to be very careful because what controlled them will control you, if you are not renewed and changed and delivered.

You will try to control others on the same basis because you have been programmed to abuse. You have been programmed to "not be loved." You have been programmed to hate. You have been programmed to have Bitterness. You have been programmed to have Envy and Jealousy. You have been programmed to have Rejection. You have been programmed to have Unloving spirits. You have been programmed to have Fear. Those who programmed you through abuse, were programmed themselves in their generations. So what are you going to do about it?

You are now a medium yourself if you are not delivered. Even if you love God, are born again and are filled with the Spirit of God, can you recognize sometimes there is a battle raging within you that wants to cause you to make someone else a victim in word or deed?

That is the programming of your spirit and your soul by evil spirits and by the intellectual processes of the memes that are set in place to give you a foundation of expression at the wrong time for the wrong reasons. That is your battle. That is your guilt. That is your torment. That is your Fear. That is what feeds the Unloving spirit, and that is antichrist.

It is time for you to recognize that the forces which rule the people who are rejecting you or telling you all this stuff or abusing you, that they themselves are programmed by the devil. They are unrenewed in their spirit and their soul, and they are also acting out something that is not what God created for them.

In order for you to be free to follow *a more excellent way,* you have to be able to separate people from their sin and from the motivating powers and the memes that are driving them in their ignorance, in their darkness, and in their weakness. You have to recognize they are under the control of an antichrist spirit. When you do that and you can come to that place with discernment, hopefully there is nothing else left in you that can hook up with them.

That is why deliverance and freedom are so important. Because you can have all this knowledge and you can resist the devil, but if that hasn't worked you may need more deliverance, because there may be a spirit that has just not gone. That spirit may need to be addressed and cast out of you, so that you can get on with the renewing of your mind.

You have to be able to separate yourself from the forces that have programmed mankind in death, hell and destruction from the beginning. You have to make sure there is nothing within you that is going to link up with what is in them, because that is how abuse occurs.

There is a spirit in that person who says or does something unloving. The Unloving spirits that are in you — Rejection or Bitterness or Envy and Jealousy, will pop up all of a sudden. Now you have two evil spirits having conversation with each other. That becomes your sin and the person's sin too.

When you allow yourself to be a medium of expression for evil spirits in the kingdom of the devil, you are a medium for Satan. You are a medium for an antichrist spirit that wants to exalt itself in the earth and use you as a medium of expression. When you allow that to happen, that is your sin, and it needs to be repented for. It is important that there be an antidote here.

Freedom has an open door.

The open door to freedom is recognizing, taking responsibility, repenting and turning away from sin. Recognizing, which is discerning, means taking personal responsibility for what has been done through you. Then you move on to repenting and turning away from it once and for all. When you fall, either because the spirit is there or because of unrenewed memes in your mind, what do you do?

You repent and take responsibility all over again. From day-to-day, you work out your own salvation with fear and trembling. From day-to-day, you come to a place where you are more, and more, and more free, and then you yourself can teach transgressors the error of their ways, because your own obedience has been fulfilled and the power of the Holy Spirit can come into your life unchecked.

The only thing that separates us from the fullness of the Holy Spirit in our lives is our personal sin. The Holy Spirit is not going to share turf with an antichrist spirit. Your ability to be used by God and to fellowship with God is in direct relationship to you falling out of agreement with Satan and his kingdom and every evil thought that is flowing through

147

any person, including yourself. Your mind is renewed by the washing in the water of the Word, holding every thought in captivity, casting down every false imagination.

It is the work of unraveling 6,000 years of Satan's control. It is the work of taking your life back. Freedom has always come in the world at a great cost of life and limb. Certain nations are still prepared to pay for freedom with life and limb. We are not asking you to die on a battlefield. We are not asking you to give life or limb, but we are asking you to take back the freedom of your sovereignty.

Let's understand the battle. Today, some of the great tools of medicine available to doctors are x-rays, sonograms and MRI's. They look inside you to see what is wrong without personally entering there. Those tools are tools of discernment. They are looking for things that are wrong that are causing you problems.

Through discernment in ministry we are going into you from the outside, x-raying everything that might not be right on the inside. According to Scripture, God knows everything, every dimension within your human spirit. He knows every thought you have in your soul, He knows every molecular part of your physiological body, and He even knows how many hairs you have on your head. He is omniscient, all knowing.

If our Father is all knowing, and He has already x-rayed us from spirit, soul and body, then it would be good for us, as His servants, for Him to share that with us. He has given us His Word to help us understand.

Spirit is spirit, soul is soul, and body is body, and they all must be dealt with independently. Our problems begin in the realm of the spirit with psychological and biological manifestations. The doctor ignores the spirit, and he ignores the psychology. He goes directly to allopathic medicine; he goes directly to the external problem and tries to fix it. The psychologist and the psychiatrist ignore the physiology and the spiritual and go directly to the soul and try to fix it.

The soul and the body cannot be fixed unless the spirit of man is renewed in the image of God.

I said the psychology of man and the physiology of man cannot be fixed or renewed unless the spirit of man has been restored in the image of the living God. Proverbs 23:7 says, "As the man thinketh in his heart (in his spirit), so is he."

When you have an Unloving spirit living in your human spirit, so are you. Do you like it in there? Does it make you feel good? Does it make you have a good day? Does it torment you? Does it project? Does it want to use you as a medium of antichrist in your own actions towards others? Read the rest of 1 Corinthians 13 about love. God is love!

Hebrews 4:11 says, "Let us labor therefore to enter into that rest."

Are we talking about a kind of rest for you now? Do you think you would have a better day if you did not have to struggle with the Unloving spirit, with all this Self-Pity and all these antichrist thoughts? Do you think that would be a form of rest? Let us labor therefore to enter into that rest, lest any man fall after the same example of unbelief. What will keep you from the rest we are talking about? Unbelief. Unbelief and doubt are also antichrist spirits. Without faith it is impossible to please God because God's faith represents your future. If you do not have faith for your future because of unbelief and doubt, you are eliminating God and His provision for your life, and you open the door for Fear to become the fruit of your life, which is the faith of Satan.

149

Open your hearts; open your minds. For the Word of God is Jesus Christ of Nazareth.

John says,

> In the beginning was the Word, and the Word was with God, and the Word was God.   John 1:1

There is a prophetic picture of Christ coming in Revelation:

> [11]And I saw heaven opened, and behold a white horse; and he that sat upon him *was* called Faithful and True, and in righteousness he doth judge and make war.
>
> [12]His eyes *were* as a flame of fire, and on his head *were* many crowns; and he had a name written, that no man knew, but he himself.
>
> [13]And he *was* clothed with a vesture dipped in blood: and his name is called The Word of God.
>
> [14]And the armies *which were* in heaven followed him upon white horses, clothed in fine linen, white and clean.
>   Revelation 19:11-14

So who is the army? Zechariah says the saints are the army.

> And ye shall flee *to* the valley of the mountains; for the valley of the mountains shall reach unto Azal: yea, ye shall flee, like as ye fled from before the earthquake in the days of Uzziah king of Judah: and the LORD my God shall come, *and* all the saints with thee.   Zechariah 14:5

Who is a saint? You! Get on with being a saint; quit being an ain't. The only difference between a saint and an ain't is the letter "s." It stands for salvation and the Savior. So how do you go from being an ain't to a saint? Add salvation and the Savior. What does the word Jesus mean? Savior. Salvation. Add Jesus to your life and you are no longer an ain't, but you are a saint. Say, "I ain't an ain't, I is a saint." That is bad English, but it is true anyway. Amen.

Hebrews 4:12 says, "For the Word of God (Jesus), is quick and powerful and sharper than any two-edged sword." Do you know what a two-edged sword is? I used to be in the sharpening business and people would bring me bayonets, swords and knives to sharpen for them. When you thrust a two-edged sword, you never have to make another move because as the victim moves, it continues to cut. This is used as an example of war. The Word of God is sharper than a two-edged sword that has that cutting edge from the point on both sides of the blade.

But the Word of God is sharper than a two-edged sword, piercing even to the *uniting*? This is where I break with integration and fusion. Integration and fusion is not a dividing of the soul and spirit; it is a uniting of the soul and the spirit. It takes the past and makes it part of the present and the future as a form of cohabitation, integrating the components of your past into your present.

However the Scriptures say the Word of God comes to *divide* the spirit from the soul. When you have been bound by generations of an antichrist attack on you as an Unloving spirit, you have become one in the spirit with that type of abuse and that type of unloveliness. It is reinforced by an Unloving spirit within your spirit to make sure you stay that way. You are one with the nature of Satan in that area of your life. The Word of God is supposed to *divide* the spirit from the soul so that the Word of God can come in to bring you *a more excellent way*, to bring you a concept that is far superior and represents creation from the beginning for your life. You are going to have to first get right spiritually, and then your soul can be renewed by the very Word that came to separate.

That is the same Word you meditate on, and as you take that Word, you munch on it like a cow chewing its cud. It

151

becomes part of you, and you are grinding away, listening to tapes and reading your Bible. This is work. It keeps grinding, and grinding away, and finally you produce milk one day. I guess that's why the Word of God is called the milk of the Word. You do not get milk unless the cow chews and processes it over, and over, and over, and over, and over. That is work. If I were a cow, I would not want to have to do that. I would just eat my grass and give milk. But that is not what God designed in order to produce milk. So it is a miracle that milk comes, anyway.

So from the understanding of the spirit and the soul, the Unloving spirit within your spirit controls you from that dimension, and you have become one with its way of thinking in all of your life. It has been reinforced by people who also had it — people who were victims and now have made you a victim. The plan is this: to make sure you do the same in your lifetime. That is why you are tormented.

The Word of God comes to separate the soul from the spirit and the joints and the marrow (that would be for physical healing), and is a discerner of the thoughts and intents of the heart. What motivates you? Is it an antichrist spirit or is it the Holy Spirit that has filled that void with truth? The Holy Spirit cannot give you power unless you first have the Word of God in you because the Holy Spirit only acts on the Word of God. So if you want the power of God in your life you have to have the Word of God in your life, because the Holy Spirit does not speak of Himself, He only executes the will of the Father and honors the Word of God through Jesus Christ.

> **Howbeit when he, the Spirit of truth, is come, he will guide you into all truth: for he shall not speak of himself; but whatsoever he shall hear, *that* shall he speak: and he will shew you things to come.** John 16:13

So if you want the Holy Spirit to be with you, He is called the Spirit of truth. Jesus said it was important for Him to go away so He could send the Comforter, who is the Holy Spirit.

> **Nevertheless I tell you the truth; It is expedient for you that I go away: for if I go not away, the Comforter will not come unto you; but if I depart, I will send him unto you.**
> John 16:7

The Holy Spirit is not a force; He is a person of the Godhead. When the Spirit of truth is come, He shall lead you into all truth. Jesus said this, to know the truth, and the truth will make you free.

> **And ye shall know the truth, and the truth shall make you free.**
> John 8:32

Truth is the foundation for discernment from God.

That is why in Hebrews 5:14 it says, "Those able to handle strong meat are those who by reason of exercise of their senses are able to discern, discern, discern, both good and evil." Is that Unloving spirit which is bugging you good or evil? God intended discernment to begin with yourself first, not with someone external who will tell you what is wrong with you. If you can't discern it for yourself, then there are administrations of the kingdom of God through Jesus Christ, through the fivefold ministry and the gifts of the Holy Spirit, which God has placed in the church to help you spiritually to get over this hump. God is able to do that through people.

I am a gift to you from Jesus the Word. If I am a gift to you from Jesus the Word, what am I supposed to be doing for you? I am supposed to be giving you the Word; I am supposed to be giving you everything that He is. Everything that He is, the Father is. The antichrist spirit must be broken

153

so that the Spirit of Christ, the Spirit of the Father and the Holy Spirit can dwell within you forever as truth and as a Comforter, so that the Scriptures may be fulfilled: for as many as are led by the Spirit of God, they are the sons of God.

> **For as many as are led by the Spirit of God, they are the sons of God.** Romans 8:14

Let God be true and every man or woman who has abused you a liar! Do not listen to it any longer; cast it down. Who are you? You are not who they told you you were. Do you know there are people who are trained assassins, character assassins? *Antagonist in the Church* is a book that describes people set in place by the devil to come into churches and cause trouble by destroying pastors, marriages and sheepfolds. That is a goat. There is a spirit behind it that wants destruction. Romans 12:18 says, if at all possible, live peaceably. But if you have an antichrist, Unloving spirit, it will engineer destruction. It will engineer grief, and it will engineer strife. It will cause trouble because it must be fulfilled in its nature to use you as a vehicle for Satan, to create chaos and destruction and the elements of pain.

Hebrews 4:12 says, dividing asunder the soul and the spirit, of the joints and marrow, and is a discerner of the thoughts and intents…

Behind the thought there may be an evil intent.

What is the motivation? Satan has programmed you and your families for destruction. He has done it by doing to you what he wants you to do to others. The fertile foundation is the Bitterness, the Envy and Jealousy, the Rejection, the Unloving spirits and the Fear. He is banking on the fact that what destroyed your mommy and daddy, and your grandmommy, and granddaddy, is going to destroy you, and you are going to do the same thing to your children.

You can program your children to be unloved. You can program them to be hated. You can program them to be driven. You can program them to be rejected. You can program them to be an extension of death, hell and destruction, because that is what the Unloving spirit is up to. That is its intent through you, to not allow you to be loved. If it does not allow you to be loved, you can't possibly love your neighbor, and if you can't love your neighbor, it has already created a fruit. Your neighbor feels rejected by you, feels unloved by you, feels like you do not love them, you do not care for them, all because you already are a puppet on a string, being controlled by the programming of Satan in your life.

It is time for you to have a reality check. It is time for you to separate yourself in the spiritual dimension of your life, to understand, to use discernment, and to recognize that you are not double minded. You are not a fragmented, split personality because Christ is not divided, and Christ is not split. You must put on the mind of Christ. There is no double mindedness in Christ, because He is the Word of God. That is why you need to be filled with the knowledge of God, the Word of God. You need to believe what it says about you, and you need to believe what it tells you to do. It is for your betterment and it is for the betterment of your protégé in your generations.

There are two bodies in the earth: the body of Christ and the body of sin. Both are found in Scripture. The body of Christ is made up of many members. The body of sin is made up of many members. The body of Christ is made up of men and women of God redeemed by the blood of Jesus Christ, filled with the Holy Spirit and standing as light and

155

salt in the midst of a dying, evil, darkened world. The body of sin is made up of individuals just like you, but they are ruled and motivated through the spirit of Satan and his kingdom.

A double minded man is half God
and half devil in his thinking.

The world and the church are no different when it comes to insanity and biological disease; they have become one. Our home church, Pleasant Valley Church, stands for the kingdom of God and the body of Christ. There are various forms of Satanism in the earth. Self-Pity is a satanic spirit. Not loving yourself is a satanic mentality. The root of all Satanism is self-hatred, self-rejection and self-abuse. The spirit of antichrist promotes disobedience to God, not accepting and loving yourself, and promotes the kingdom of Self — me, me, my, my. "He that would be greatest among you, is he that would be the servant of all."

But he that is greatest among you shall be your servant.
Matthew 23:11

So much for self-exaltation. So much for supremacy.

Isaiah 58 says the beginning of all healing is not just how much you say you love God or how much you worship in the sanctuary.

The fast you have been called to
is service to others.

Isaiah 58:8 says, "Then your health shall spring forth speedily." Jesus did not have an antichrist spirit, because when He was dying on the cross in a selfless way for us He said, "Father forgive them for they know not what they do." In His dying breaths He saved someone and preached the gospel to him right on the cross. He said, "This day you shall be with me in Paradise." What a way to go. Forgiving and saving and caring.

The Unloving spirit won't allow you to save another, won't allow you to care for another, and won't allow you to care for yourself. It may come in religious ways. It may come through charities, which many times are an appeasement of the conscience. There are many sincere people who give to charities, and God bless them. It is not what you do; it is who you are.

In Hebrews 4:12 it says, "The Word of God is quick and powerful, sharper than a two-edged sword, and is a discerner of the thoughts and intents of the heart. Neither is there any creature that is not manifest in his sight, but all things are naked and opened unto the eyes of him with whom we have to do." This is one of the most powerful scriptures on discernment in the Bible. The Word of God is a discerner of the thoughts and intents of the heart. What do you think that creature is in verse 13? We are discerning every invisible principality and power that answers to Satan himself. Those are the creatures. They are wide open. They are naked. They are manifest before His eyes, and they are well-seen and well-known. You should know them as well as He does because you are His children.

Do you think I tell my children what to watch out for? Watch out for this. Watch out for that. This is what a scorpion looks like. This is what a rattlesnake looks like. If you see this, do not go. Do this; do that. Avoid here; avoid there. When the rattlesnake is coiled, do not try to pet its head just because the head is up. Do not do what my son did, just sit down in a pile of leaves in the ditch and not look to see if a scorpion is sitting in the leaves. When we first came here, he sat down in the ditch, and there was a scorpion that nailed him right on his butt. Well, the

157

scorpions around here won't kill you; they just basically feel like a bee sting. He hurt for an hour or so, and then it was over with. But now he has good discernment. Before he sits down, he looks to see where he is sitting.

Do we have to be bitten by the enemy before we have discernment, or should we have discernment before we are bitten? The antichrist spirit will allow you to get bitten, time and time again, and still no have discernment. How many times do you struggle with feelings of unloveliness about yourself?

The battle is on two dimensions: the spiritual dimension and your own memory. You have been trained and you have been forced into a place of unrenewal by your enemy and your family trees. The Unloving spirit has come because your ancestors did not love and did not care one for another. They either abandoned you or did not love you.

Psychology has become our religion, even in the Christian church. Where psychology bumps up against the Scriptures, psychology is now the rule, not the Scriptures. We are in trouble concerning the purity of God in our lives; we are a mixture. The world is out of order, but we must seek God to retain our sanity.

Have you finally come to the conclusion that if you do not love yourself, you have an Unloving spirit and now you know why? Had you ever thought about the fact that self-hatred, self-rejection and an Unloving spirit toward yourself are antichrist spirits designed to separate you from God, yourself and others?

Had you ever thought about the fact that you have been programmed to hate? Had you considered that you have been programmed to be rejected, to be unloved, to compete, to fail or to win, or to perform? You have been programmed to do many things that had nothing to do with God's plans for your life. You need to think about it because if you have been programmed to be a medium of evil because evil was done to you, then the chances of you being an extension of that against someone else is very good. This is the rollover. This is what I call spiritual genetics.

SPIRITUAL GENETICS

You know what biological genetics are, but have you ever considered spiritual genetics? That would not be the genes literally, but it is a metaphor used to describe the inherited familiar spirits. The inherited familiar spirits would be the spiritual genetics of your life. There are two dimensions of how your enemy can program you for your generation to be the opposite of who God created you to be. The first would be biological or physiological genetically inherited problems and diseases or psychologically inherited diseases. The other is the inheritance of familiar spirits. Jungian psychology would call those the archetypes and dark shadows that you were born with. In Ephesians 6:12 the Bible calls them devils, principalities and powers, spiritual wickedness in high places and the rulers of the darkness of this world.

My job as a shepherd is to restore you to God and to give you back your life as He intended for you to have it from the beginning. This is the first day of the rest of your life. When I read about the great men and women of God in the Bible, age was never an issue. Some of the greatest men and women of God were over 60, 70 or 80 years of age before they even started in ministry. Don't buy this programming of your mind that you have to retire at age 60.

In psychological diseases we can give you two examples: inherited spiritual insanity and inherited biological insanity.

Insanity can be inherited both from the spiritual standpoint and also from the biological standpoint. Coming out of conflicts of the soul, manic depression is a genetically inherited disease, but paranoid schizophrenia is a spiritually inherited disease. Here are two examples in the area of the soul or the thinking. Both of those diseases are the result of an imbalance of the neurotransmitters that cause the process of electrical transmission of thought. Your soul is the composite of genetics, chemistry and electricity (nerve processes). You think you have it together, but you are vulnerable; your enemy knows you are vulnerable.

For example, manic depression is the result of an underproduction of serotonin, which is a facilitator of thought, whereas paranoid schizophrenia is an overproduction of serotonin in addition to overproduction of norepinephrine. So here we have two psychological diseases. Manic depression is set in place to permanently create the undersecretion of serotonin by a genetic factor, the recessive gene to the mother, and the X chromosome. Paranoid schizophrenia is set in place through a familiar spirit of life circumstances coming out of the following: Rejection, Fear, and rebellion, in that order. These are able to trigger the overproduction of serotonin and norepinephrine producing a breakdown in your ability to process thought and your ability to come to a place that we call normalcy. The Unloving spirit is a key component of insanity.

Manic depression – underproduction of serotonin
Paranoid schizophrenia – overproduction of serotonin

All insanity is either a result of involvement with Occultism or abuse or a combination of both. You think you have control of your faculties. You do to a certain degree, but there are various forces, including your enemy, that want you. When you think how Satan tempted Eve, he tempted her at the level of thought, in her thinking. When

Satan came to Jesus to tempt Him, he tempted Him at the level of intellectual thought, in his thinking. What does Fear do to you? It attacks you at the level of intellectual thought, in our thinking, by impressions and imaginations and projections. That is why there can be no inner healing or emotional healing unless the spiritual dynamics have been straightened out. Inner healing is just a Band-Aid. It does two things: renew the memes or memories, and let the spirit still stay there. Psychology tries to redirect the thinking and the memes and have you come into a place of understanding it better and cohabiting with it better, but it does not remove the spiritual dynamics.

THE STRATEGIES

You cannot remove an evil spirit by counseling it; that is unscriptural. You either have to resist it, walk away from it, or cast it out. You may be able to defeat the Unloving, unclean spirit just by the truth that is coming to you in this teaching, and you won't need deliverance. You may also defeat that Unloving, unclean spirit that is within you by a process of resisting and holding every thought captive over time, until you learn to make it submit to you so that you rule over it. You stand on its poor little head and squash it, and you keep on moving away from it. You just may need deliverance.

There are three phases. First, know the truth; the truth will make you free. Second, resist the devil and he will flee. Third, cast the evil spirits out. All three can be independent of each other and can be as complete as any one of the others.

You need to get balance in this thing. There are only three ways to deal with evil spirits. First, Johns 8:32 says that to know the truth brings freedom, because the truth will make you free. The truth gives you the ability to decide what is good and evil, and that is discernment. Through discernment you can defeat every evil spirit in your life. I don't care how much it squeals and screams in your ears; you can subject it in the power of the Holy Spirit.

The second area is resist the devil and he shall flee. That is what we call spiritual warfare, a life application of having discernment and going into resistance. This is where the first four R's to freedom come in. First, Resistance involves Recognition. That Recognition would be discernment. Second is taking Responsibility. That would be turning away from it, falling out of agreement with it. Third is Repentance. Fourth is Removing it. Run away from it, get away from it, get it out of your life, and subdue it.

You are learning how to apply truth to your life. You hold every thought in captivity, come to a place where you ask God to help you, and there's prayer. You would be surprised how a simple prayer will change you. Rather than going down under it why not say, "God, help me, please." Rather than saying, "Oh my, I have a spiritual headache, I am going down under it," why not come up in the midst of it and say, "God, help me." Get someone else to pray for you. Ask them: "Please pray for me." All you have to do if you are asked "What's the problem?" is say, "I am down under it." "Well, in the name of Jesus, be on top of it, Amen." It could be that simple. James 5:16 says, "The fervent, effectual prayer of a righteous man or woman availeth much."

The Unloving spirit is something that you either inherited or are programmed with by someone. You inherited it as an evil spirit, or it was programmed into you because you were victimized by those who were supposed to care for you and love you. The greatest impact that Satan has over you is for someone to victimize you and abuse you who God has set over you, who you are supposed to look up to and trust as a point of reference. That is the ultimate searing and scarring of the human spirit because it involves the element of trust. It is impossible to love others if you can't trust them.

Now it could be that distrust may be your problem, and they may have done nothing wrong. We're not talking about that type of distrust. If you already have distrust, there are not too many people who can survive it. If you already have the spirit of distrust, others could do everything perfect around you, and you still would not trust them because an Unloving spirit produces distrust. First John 4:18 has four parts to it:

> **There is no fear in love; but perfect love casteth out fear: because fear hath torment. He that feareth is not made perfect in love.** 1 John 4:18

"There is no Fear in love." We are not talking about Fear right now, but we are talking about love, loving ourselves. But what does 1 John 4:18 say? There is no Fear in love.

If Fear is there, love is not.

You may already have an Unloving spirit, and you may already have distrust. You may already have that distrust to the degree that if Jesus walked into the room you probably would not trust Him.

"There is no Fear in love. Perfect love casts out Fear." You are learning how to receive perfect love. Love one another! You ought to be loving on one another. If you see someone walking around, instead of withdrawing in distrust, you ought to say, "You know what? I sure love you today; let me give you a big squeeze." You ought to be building each other up in love instead of saying, "What happened to you? Did you have a rough night?" Wait a minute now, where are you coming from?

If it is that obvious that someone had a rough night, rather than enhancing that battle, in the great fantastic discernment you just had about him having a rough night, why not raise him up? Instead of going up to him with your truth, why not go up with wisdom? The wisdom of God would say, "You know what? I sure appreciate you. We are all overcoming things and having our victories. I just want you to know you are loved and God loves you, and I am praying for you. Can I give you a big squeeze this morning to encourage you and exhort you to have a wonderful day?" Now is that better wisdom than discernment? Discernment without wisdom is sometimes still a problem. The Bible says in Galatians 6, "If a brother be overtaken in a fault (or had a rough night), those of you who consider yourself spiritual restore such a one in the spirit of meekness, lest you be tempted in like manner (and have a rough night tomorrow yourself)." Love one another!

"Fear hath torment." When you have an Unloving spirit that's coming from a breach in a relationship with someone who was supposed to nurture you and care for you, there is a torment that comes which is incredible. That torment is what produces all insanity and shades and variations of it. That type of torment is what fuels the mind-body connection. That is the torment that nags at you and accuses you to yourself. That is the Unloving spirit.

Part four of 1 John 4:18 says he that feareth (because of having the Unloving spirit), is not able to accept love and give it without Fear. He has not received the perfect love that would cast out Fear and the Unloving spirit. He that feareth is not made perfect in love himself. If you have all these ingredients, that means you are unable to give and receive love without Fear yourself. Now we have the rollover, and you have been programmed to "not be able" to give and receive love without Fear and to be tormented in the spiritual and psychological dimensions of your life. You have to prepare yourself to stand before God as an equal partner with Christ in creation. He came to redeem you from the curse and to save your soul because He loves you.

Our generation is programmed to do evil. New comic books for children have violent superheroes. Soap operas program you to hate your husbands, to have strife in families, to scream and holler at each other. They program you into deception, division, hatred, marital strife, adultery and fornication. When you feed on that you are programmed with the same suspicions, and you wonder why you look at your mate with suspicion. You need to be alert to what you yield your eyes, your ears and your five physical senses to. Silence is an affirmation of evil when you are confronted with it. If you say, "I just don't want to get involved," you are already involved if you are there and you don't voice an opposite vote.

Romans says,

> **Now I beseech you, brethren, mark them which cause divisions and offences contrary to the doctrine which ye have learned; and avoid them.**   Romans 16:17

If you find someone who is trying to cause trouble and gossip, going behind the scenes to separate brothers and sisters in the Lord through innuendo, you have a division-maker on your hands, and you have trouble. If we had taken a stand in our generations, to stand up against those members of our own homes and tell them to either get it together and love us or get out of our face, we would have solved the problem a long time ago.

A lot of people struggle with the law, because the law under Moses in the Old Testament church said if you did certain things against your neighbor, you would be killed and stoned by sundown. God put that in the law, first of all to eradicate evil from the midst of God's people, and secondly, to put godly fear in those who would be evil and show that this would happen to them. It almost always solved the problem.

You need to take a stand against victimization. The Bible says, "If at all possible, live peaceably one with another." It got so bad in my home when I was a senior in high school; I had to go live with a friend and his family. I had to walk away from it. At that time I did not understand that I was taking a stand against evil because I was traumatized in it, but I had to do it.

In ministry, we have made a firm commitment to people who are victims in relationships, either emotionally, verbally, physically or sexually. That commitment is that if we can't save two people in that relationship, we are going to save one. There is no reason why both people should go down and drown in the sea of hell over a spiritual issue that is making one person a victim. Do you think it is God's will that both people should die in victimization, or do you think we should save one of them? We take a firm stand against abuse in any form because it is ungodly. What the Bible says is this, where there is strife there are evil things (James 3:16). You need to listen to the Word.

Everything that violates what the Scriptures say about a subject is antichrist. Everything that matches the Scriptures completely in content and with the correct spirit behind it, is the mind of Christ. You should have the mind of Christ because He is the Word of God. He is the Creator of all things, visible and invisible. Would you rather follow the voice of the Creator, or would you like to follow the voice of the destroyer? Which voice do you want to follow: the voice of the Shepherd or the voice of the goat?

OCCULTISM

Do you want to follow the voice of Jesus the Christ or do you want to follow the voice of Mendes the goat? The five-pointed star turned upside down on the back of the Freemason's car is Baphomet, the goat of Mendes, which is a caricature of Satan himself. The horns are the horns of a goat. The one pointing down is the hair of his chin. Wherever it is found, the five-pointed star is an occultic symbol. If you put it in a circle, you have a way to conjure up demons. An occultic star directs light for an occultic purpose. It is occultic because a true star emanates light in 360 degrees. You will find a true star on compasses. There are four points: north, south, east and west, with light radiating in every degree around it. Light radiates in 360 degrees.

When you study the origin of the occultic star, you will find Satanism and the occult without exception. The occultic star is the star of Remphan found in Acts 7:43. Basically it is an inverted triangle superimposed upon a triangle and is commonly called the Star of David, but David did not have a star. Solomon did in his apostasy, when he worshipped the pagan gods of his wives and concubines.

The Washington Monument is the famous phallic symbol coming out of Freemasonry. The star of the god Remphan was rebirthed by the Rothschilds as the goat of Mendes. The star of the god Remphan was the star of Occultism in the pagan nations in Judaism. The Rothschilds were a prominent family from Germany, and they changed their name from Von Braun to Rothschild and took this occultic symbol as

167

their coat of arms. Rothschild literally means red shield. It is a red coat of arms. Today the Rothschilds are world famous, especially in Israel. In the changing of the guard in 1948, when the Jews took back their land from the Arabs and the Palestinians, this symbol came with the Rothschilds, who went from Germany into Israel. It was later adopted by the Jewish Red Cross. Later the color was changed to blue, and in 1949 or 1950, it became their symbol for a couple of decades. Finally the Jewish government changed its name to the Star of David, and thus it became a part of the national flag of Israel.

Israel today is occultic. They are supposed to be God's people, but they will accept the false messiah in the future in their Occultism, and the Star of David is the symbol of their Occultism. So if you add anything Christian to that symbol, like the dove and the cross, you are Christianizing Occultism and wearing it as a symbol. This is a spiritual, occultic pride.

TAKE YOUR LIFE BACK

The point we are making is that you can be influenced and programmed from many quarters. Are you ready to take your life back? What is going to happen when that Unloving spirit crops up and starts throwing Bitterness, Envy and Jealousy, and Rejection all through you? Are you going to believe it? Are you going to act on it? It wants you to, and you will if you are not careful in your resisting stage of warfare. It is very good at throwing flash cards at you. It will hold up a flash card from the past of a word; it will even hit the start button on a video that will roll through your mind, reinforcing what someone did to you from the past so that it can let you forget who you are in Christ. It tries to reinforce that antichrist mentality that you are rejected, you are evil, and you are no good. It wants you to believe it so

168

you will start to act on it. You have to have the mind of Christ.

The mind of Christ says you are a new creature, a new creation. You are loved of God. You are not rejected, and you are going to have to take that position, stand on it, believe in it, and let God be true because He said that about you.

Let every man be a liar who disagrees with the Word of God. You have to take that stand! When the programming demons come out of people, trying to trash you and reject you, you are going to have to understand they have the antichrist spirit, and they do not know who you are in Christ. They themselves are separated from the living God by an antichrist spirit that is Unloving. Why is an Unloving spirit called an antichrist spirit? In 1 John 3, it says God is love. John 3:16 says, "God so loved the world that He gave..."

An Unloving spirit is antichrist because it defies the very nature of God. If you have been created in His image, you are love, not in the New Age term. Your nature is love; your nature is to forgive. Your nature is to give love to others and to receive it for yourself. If it doesn't come back to you when you are giving it (because they have an Unloving, antichrist spirit in them), it does not make any difference because they are not your source.

God the Father is your source, the Lord Jesus Christ is your source, and the Holy Spirit is your source. If you stand complete in the Godhead, nothing can touch you no matter how vicious, how ugly and how defiling it is. Stand complete in the security of who you are in God; that is the mind of Christ.

Jesus showed you the love of the Father. Jesus showed you that even to death and the cross. Jesus put His trust in the Father because of love and trust. God allowed Jesus to die such a horrible death because mankind is already dying a horrible death. Jesus came to take that into His body so that it could be paid once and for all. He became one of us. He took the sins of the world and everything that it represented, including murder and death. He bore it as a sacrificial Lamb so the penalty of the curse could be fulfilled through Him.

You can be free by believing in Him.

You don't have to be rejected any longer because you aren't rejected. Self has to be broken. "Self" is the nature of Satan through principalities and powers that have ingrained themselves with your spirit and your memes and have programmed you to be hated and unloved. If you are not careful, you will be set up in league with other people who will do the same thing to you. That is what produces bad marriages. Two familiar spirits got married. We are so busy quoting Matthew 19:6 that says, "What God put together, let no man put asunder." Who said God put it together? You know the story about that guy who went and got drunk one night and woke up the next morning married and wondered why he had a marriage problem for five years.

It is time to wake up, to have the mind of Christ, to be men and women of God and to take your place in the earth free. John 8:36 says, "He whom the son makes free is free indeed."

Ephesians 4:23 and 5:26 say that you are renewed in your mind by the washing of the water of the Word. You need to be deprogrammed from the thinking of Satan for destruction, and you need to be renewed in your mind to receive the life of God your Father, through Jesus Christ, for your freedom. You need to be as committed to that as God was committed to making it possible for you. You need to be as committed to your freedom as you can be. You need to take a stand and say, "I am not going to think destruction anymore!"

You are either part of the solution, or you are part of the pollution. You are either feeding life, or you are feeding destruction. Christ is life; Satan is destruction. When you have the mind of Christ, you have the Word of God. Wisdom comes and uses that knowledge to produce a way of life for you.

In 1 Corinthians 12, the gift of knowledge ties the past to the present, but the gift of wisdom takes the present and moves it to the future. When it is happening, it just flows. As the Holy Spirit wills, it comes forth. Whether it be discerning of spirits, the gift of miracles, the gift of healing, whether it be tongues or interpretation of prophecy, the gift of faith or whether it be the gift of knowledge or the gift of wisdom, it is all there.

The gift of knowledge brings you from your past and establishes the present. The gift of wisdom takes what the knowledge has brought you and propels you into the future according to that knowledge. Both of those gifts are used to establish you now. They deal with the past and present, moving you to the future with the mind of Christ in the direction of the Holy Spirit. That is the fruit of the gift of knowledge and the gift of wisdom.

The prophet brings insight to a person's life. If I read my Bible correctly, it was the prophet who brought the people knowledge, no one else. The knowledge about Paul being bound in Jerusalem was given by the prophet, not an ordinary believer.

> And when he was come unto us, he took Paul's girdle, and bound his own hands and feet, and said, Thus saith the Holy Ghost, So shall the Jews at Jerusalem bind the man that owneth this girdle, and shall deliver *him* into the hands of the Gentiles.
> Acts 21:11

Many people misunderstand. There is so much divination in the church today; you do not know whether it is God or the devil talking. The only way you can understand is to compare the scriptural pattern of the Bible to what is now being said. Then you just have to open your heart up to God and say, "God, You have to confirm this or reject it, one or the other." Do not go there in Fear, but go there according to discernment. Try the spirits whether or not they are of God. Amen?

> Beloved, believe not every spirit, but try the spirits whether they are of God: because many false prophets are gone out into the world.
> 1 John 4:1

You also have to be wary of flatterers. Do you know what the Bible says about flatterers? Psalm 78:36 says they are going to eat your lunch real soon. They come to you and pat you on the back and say how wonderful you are and flatter you.

There's nothing wrong with telling someone something nice about themselves, but you've seen what I mean by people who just come around with syrup and make you feel uncomfortable. When you have that uncomfortable feeling about someone who is just rushing you with this gooey stuff, you need to listen to the Holy Spirit warning you to get away. But if someone comes up and says, "You know I like that outfit on you today. You look really nice." That does not make you feel uncomfortable because that is not flattery; that is a compliment. There is a different spirit behind a compliment than the one behind flattery. Read what your Bible says about flattery in Proverbs.

172

Establish your feet in a direction of action. That action must come from the resolve that you are going to make up your mind to accept yourself and stop hating yourself starting right now. You are going to fall out of agreement; you are going to recognize it. You will be responsible in it as you repent to God for those areas where you have not accepted yourself, and then you run from it.

Get away from it, and do not make it part of your life. When it comes knocking on your heart's door about three days down the road and says, "I am the Unloving spirit. I am here to tell you and to remind you that you are a hypocrite, you old ugly thing you. I will remind you about some things about yourself if you will listen to me." Reject it. Put your feet down and say, "Wait a minute. Get away from me. Get behind me Satan." What did Jesus say? "Get thee behind me Satan." What does that mean? It means, "Okay, Mr. Big Guy, I hear what you are saying, but just step aside. I'm moving on in my life. I'm moving on in God. I'm moving on because I have the mind of Christ. I'm moving on!"

You resist the devil when you say, "Satan get behind me." You have this person interrupting the flow of the mind of Christ and who God has called you to be, and you bump right into him. He is talking to you, chewing your ears off, and you start to listen. Do not listen! Say, "Excuse me. You are in my road. Get behind me Satan; I'm moving on." He will be chewing your ears off while he is walking behind you because he never shuts up. Do you know why? The Bible says in Revelation, "The accuser of the brethren is cast down, who accused them before their God day and night."

> And I heard a loud voice saying in heaven, Now is come salvation, and strength, and the kingdom of our God, and the power of his Christ: for the accuser of our brethren is cast down, which accused them before our God day and night.
>
> Revelation 12:10

173

When you hear the accusations in your mind, you are going to hear them day and night until you become free of them. But quit listening to them and get on with being that man or woman of God with the mind of Christ. Your enemy will accuse you, but you can have victory over him. You can get on with your life, and you can be victorious. In a lot of areas you can become totally free and never have that problem again.

There are many areas of my life where I used to have to do spiritual warfare that I no longer have to. It's just a completed work in my heart, and the devil doesn't have access to me. When he comes to me, there's just nothing in there he can grab hold of. Are there some areas of your life that are a finished work? The same thing that produced that finished work in that area of your life is the same thing that will produce additional areas of finished work in your life. So let God do His work. It means freedom to you, and it means peace to you. It means less Fear to you, it means less torment to you, and it means less feelings of being unloved to you.

THE ARMOR

Now we will address the armor that the Unloving spirit uses to reinforce himself. Remember Luke 11:21-22 says, "When the strong man armed keepeth his palace, his goods are in peace. When anyone stronger comes upon him, he takes from him all his armor in which he trusted and spoileth his goods." Are you tired of being spoiled by the devil? Are you ready to spoil him for a while? Do you know how you give an evil spirit a headache? By identifying him and bringing him into light. It just cannot stand the light. They cannot stand truth because it exposes evil spirits.

Hebrews 4:13 says, "Neither is there any creature that is not manifest in his sight, but all things are naked and open unto him whom we have to do." Do you want to give your enemy a headache? Turn the light on. Do you know what the antidote to the devil is? It is truth, knowing the truth. When you know the truth, the truth will make you free. Discerning of spirits is one of the nine gifts of the Holy Spirit in 1 Corinthians 12. Paul said in Hebrews 5:14, if you are able to handle strong meat you are a mature man or woman of God by reason of what? Having their senses exercised to discern both good and evil.

You have to get these scriptures in your heart because your safety is the Word of God. This is the antidote, the Word of God. The mind of Christ is the Word of God. The Word of God is the sword of the Spirit. If you are trying to fight spiritual warfare, you must have the Word of God tucked away in your heart. Jesus defeated the devil with the Word of God: with the very Word that He spoke through the Holy Spirit to David in Psalms, with the very Word that He gave directly to Moses on Mount Sinai in Deuteronomy, and that is the very Word that He quoted to Satan in His day of temptation.

The sword of the Spirit — For it is written!

In ministry, when evil spirits would talk to me through people, argue with me, debate with me and quote me Scripture, do you know what I would do with that evil spirit that has the audacity to have a discussion with me? I have the mind of Christ; I have the Holy Spirit. When I hear this thing speaking to me, I say, "Yes, but over here it says, 'For it is written, for it is written.' " Even Satan has to bow his knee to the one who says what is written.

Hebrews 4:12-13 says that the sword of the Spirit is sharper than a two-edged sword, is able to penetrate even to the joint and marrow, is a discerner of the thoughts and intents of the heart and is able to separate the soul from the spirit. Neither is there any creature that is not made known or opened, discerned before him with whom we have to do.

You have to have the Word of God. You do not have to get it word-for-word. You can look it up later. The devil will run from you even if you paraphrase it. I can hear the devil now, "You didn't quote that right." "Really, well let me find it over here. Where is my concordance?"

Do you want to win your battle? Then stand up and be a man or woman of God with the mind of Christ, and get the antichrist spirit out of you. Every voice that disagrees with the mind of Christ is antichrist. You can't defeat your enemy with anything other than the Word of God. You need to know who you are. You are a king and a priest of the future. Stand up and start taking dominion over the kingdom that you are going to rule over one day! What a wonderful time to practice now by faith, according to the Word. Stand up; quit listening to lies. Every voice that disagrees with the Word of God has an antichrist spirit behind it. It is the mind of Satan, but we are told to put on the mind of Christ. He is the Word of God.

You do not have the mind of Christ if you do not know the Word. You can only defeat your enemy to the degree you have the Word tucked away in your heart, because the Word of God is the sword of the Spirit. For every voice that comes to you, you ought to be able to find a scripture in the Bible that disagrees with it. Find yourself a scripture in the Word of God that you can use against that voice that is tormenting you and accusing you. For every voice that comes from Satan, there is a Scripture that deals with it. Ecclesiastes 1:9 says, "There is nothing new under the sun," so every voice that comes is an old voice.

God has given you His Word, and He wants you to be able to use it. That is why the devil does not want you to read your Bible. Then when you do, you start yawning. Satan does not want you to put on the mind of Christ because if you do, you will slash him to pieces. You need to learn to love yourself as God has loved you.

When we get into the armor of the Unloving spirit, we are not just going to go into discernment. We are going to strip it of its armor, piece-by-piece, evil spirit by evil spirit, every bit of the evil armor that reinforces the Unloving spirit in your life.

When we name it by name, we are going to identify it, reject it, repent for it and command it to leave. The personality of an Unloving spirit is a legion, not just one evil spirit. Unless you bind the strong man, you cannot spoil his house. In Luke 11 it says the strong man armed keepeth his palace and his goods. That word "goods" is plural. That word "goods" means the pawns and the members of the legion that support his power in the person. His goods are at peace, and the legions (the evil spirits that make up the legion) are at peace. When one stronger than he comes upon him, he shall strip him of his armor in which he trusts. The Unloving spirit in your life, which is the antichrist spirit, is banking on the fact that there are certain principalities and powers in place that are able to keep you confused and messed up to the point that he can stay in you all the time. We want that whole group gone. We are going to identify all the armor that causes an Unloving spirit to stay.

The Unloving spirit has a principality it answers to and we have identified that principality as the antichrist spirit. The antichrist spirit defies the living God and what He created for His pleasure and for His purposes. The Unloving spirit is not the head dude. The antichrist spirit is. The

Unloving spirit is just an underling ruler, but he rules over another underling kingdom, the rulers of the darkness of this world. The Bible says, "Our battle is not against flesh and blood, but against principalities and powers." The Unloving spirit is one of those powers. The antichrist spirit is a principality, and the armor is the spiritual wickedness in high places and the rulers of the darkness of this world.

We are going to go into that kingdom, into the second heaven. We are going to go into your spiritual domain and flash the sword and carve these characters to pieces, if you would like to. Are you tired of listening to them? Are you tired of feeling yucky, are you tired of being in Fear? Are you tired of struggling with yourself and your identity? You need to know who you are in Christ.

You can shadowbox or use the sword; it is your choice. Know your Word and believe what it says. Luke says,

> **But if I with the finger of God cast out devils, no doubt the kingdom of God is come upon you.** Luke 11:20

Matthew says,

> **But if I cast out devils by the Spirit of God, then the kingdom of God is come unto you.** Matthew 12:28

So if you put the two together, the finger of God and the Spirit of God are one and the same. Saying "the power of God" is not correct because there is a difference between power and the Holy Spirit.

Let's do a little Bible study here. We can get into a New Age concept of the Holy Spirit being just a power, but He is a person. There are a lot of people running around looking for the power or the force. Matthew 12:28 says, "But if I cast out devils by the Spirit of God, then the kingdom of God is come unto you." Who is the Spirit of God? The Holy Spirit.

So is the finger of God the power of God or is it the Holy Spirit?

The Bible always explains itself. If you find a scripture about one subject, you will find that subject or that theme somewhere else in the Bible, Old or New Testament. You need to look for it. Everything is basically confirmed. Daniel and Revelation confirm each other in many, many places. It is not just that Jesus appeared and sent his angel to John on the isle of Patmos to give the book of Revelation, but much of the same information was given to Daniel about 530 to 550 years before by the Spirit of God in the dreams and visions that Daniel had as a prophet.

So let's make sure that we learn to study our Bible correctly. Of course my position as a pastor is to teach you how to study, right? Not feed you like a bunch of guppies. Have you ever been down to Wal-Mart and looked at those fish? You drop a little food on the surface of the water and those little fish will come. They don't care what is on the top; they just come up and eat it. They just open their mouths and suck it in. A lot of times as men and women of God, we don't take time to study the Word of God for ourselves. But the Bible is very clear that a workman who is not going to be ashamed is one who is able to rightly divide the Word of truth.

> **Study to shew thyself approved unto God, a workman that needeth not to be ashamed, rightly dividing the word of truth.**   2 Timothy 2:15

What does it mean to divide the Word of truth? You need to be able to understand it. If you do not know the Bible, when something comes down the tube that seems so right spiritually, you will just think, "Well, that sounds pretty good. That sounds like it might be from God. It might be all right. I will just go follow that." You need to learn to study the Word and know it. Read your Bible. Understand it.

Get a Bible that has some good historical footnotes that are accurate and does not explain God away. Get one that does not say He passed away 2,000 years ago, or that He is not able to do the same today as He did in the past. It is so much easier to preach a gospel in which there is no responsibility for healing and miracles; you just make God sovereign and whatever comes, glory to God. That is not scriptural. I am happy to believe in Jesus Christ, who is the same yesterday, today and forever.

The Holy Spirit is the power of God. He is *dunamis*.

Editor's Note: *Dunamis* is a Greek word translated as power. It is #1411 in the *Strong's Concordance*.

We need to be very careful that we teach, not the transliteration or the attribute of His person, but that He is a person. So when Jesus said this, "If I with the finger of God cast out devils, know ye this: The kingdom of God is come unto man," Jesus is saying, if I by the very person of the Holy Spirit cast out devils... How do we know that is what it means by the finger of God? We went to Matthew and proved it. There are so many people chasing power and "the force," getting into this power mentality, they forget the Godhead.

The Holy Spirit is the power of God. *God the Father willed it, God the Word said it, and God the Holy Spirit did it.* So we have the triune action of the Godhead, the will, the Word and the action.

You are the same. You have your will, your word and your action. You are created in His image. That is your life.

So you have the same capability to some degree, except that you are non-creative. In other words, you can't create

180

anything, but you are an extension of the very person of the Godhead in that you can think, you can say what you think, and you can do what you think and what you say. At least you try to do that to the best of your ability.

Luke says,

> [20]But if I with the finger of God cast out devils, no doubt the kingdom of God is come upon you.
> [21]When a strong man armed keepeth his palace, his goods are in peace:
> [22]But when a stronger than he shall come upon him, and overcome him, he taketh from him all his armour wherein he trusted, and divideth his spoils.
> [23]He that is not with me is against me: and he that gathereth not with me scattereth.   Luke 11:20-23

"When a strong man armed keepeth his palace..." That would be the ruling principality over the person's life, the evil spirit. When we use the term "strong man," it indicates a control or a rulership or an authority over someone. "Strong man armed" would be someone taking away the sovereignty of another. "When a strong man armed keepeth his palace..." That would be the control of a person's life by an evil spirit.

In other words, God created you with sovereignty and that means no evil spirit or principality should rule over you. You have been created to be spiritually free as sons and daughters of God under the authority of the Godhead. That is why Jesus Christ is called Lord. When these evil spirits come in and control your life, they become a lord to you and a ruler over your life.

You submit to them and their authority, their designs and their intent, and you come under their authority and control. So the palace is the individual's sovereign life that God created. But the "strong man armed" would be an evil spirit and principality that has taken over your house, your

181

palace and is controlling you. His goods would be in peace, and that is the armor.

For example, Bitterness is a ruling principality for the devil. Here in verse 21 it says that when a strong man armed, as in when Bitterness armed, keepeth your palace, his goods are in peace. What are his goods? Unforgiveness, resentment, rage, anger and wrath, hatred, violence and murder. These are now in peace under his authority. That is not your peace; that is his peace. When the evil spirit is within you, he is at peace and you are in torment. But when he is gone, he is in torment and you are in peace.

When the evil spirit is cast out, and when the strong man is cast out, he wanders through a dry place seeking a place of rest and finding none, returns to his original home to see if the house, the palace, is filled or empty. Then finding the house or the palace, empty, garnished, swept clean, he comes back in and brings with him seven much worse than himself, and the latter state of the man is much worse than the former state.

What does that scripture mean? It means when the evil spirit is cast out, it goes into torment. That dry place is in the second heaven, invisible, where evil spirits are when they do not inhabit a human being. They are in a place of torment because they have all these feelings.

They have all these urges. They have all the manifestation of their nature roaring through their consciousness. Evil spirits are disembodied beings. They are as real as you are, except they do not have a physical body, and they are bound to the spiritual dimension. They are neither in the earth, visible, nor are they in heaven, spiritually.

Jesus said in Luke 10:18, "I saw Satan fall like lightning from heaven." In Job 2:2, the sons of God came to present themselves before the Lord and Satan came with them. The Lord said to Satan, "Where have you been?" Satan said, "I've been walking up and down, to and fro, in the earth." He is still walking up and down the earth today as well as he did back in the days of Job. Has anyone seen him lately walking up and down the earth? No, because even Satan is a disembodied being and does not have the ability to manifest as a physical entity ever again. That is why he has to possess mankind through his evil spirits.

He, himself, is only going to possess one man personally one day, and that is the antichrist or the beast found in Daniel, the false messiah. He will enter into that individual and possess him personally. That antichrist, that false messiah will be possessed of Satan himself. That man will no longer exist as a human being; he will be insane with the mind of Satan.

When the evil spirit is in you, it wants to manifest itself by its nature. If it is Bitterness, it wants to use you to express Bitterness. When you allow it to do so, it becomes your sin. You need to repent to God for allowing it to become part of your life, for allowing an evil spirit or a principality, or spiritual wickedness in high places, or the rulers of the darkness of this world, for allowing anything but the Holy Spirit to control you, rule you and speak through you.

Otherwise you have become an oracle for the devil through his kingdom; then you can't be an oracle for God. When you start spouting off in anger and wrath, that is not even you. That is an evil spirit that has taken you over. You go down; it comes up. It uses your faculties as a medium of expression, and it fulfills its nature and is very happy to do so. But you are very unhappy and you become the victim.

As we teach our children how to be men and women of God one day, when these spirits take them over, and they get in trouble because they have broken a rule of the home or a rule of God, they need to have some type of restriction or time out or punishment. I tell them point blank, "Your personal evil spirit has done this through you, and you are the one in trouble. *It* is not in trouble; *it* is loving every minute of this and laughing at you every step of the way because it got you in trouble. *You* get the punishment; *it* gets the satisfaction. Now do you really think this is cool?"

Well, how about *you* having the satisfaction, and *it* getting the punishment? How do you punish an evil spirit? You cast it out of your life. That is its punishment. If you want to really punish an evil spirit that is walking up and down the earth or trying to control you, remove it from your life. That is the punishment that God ordained be done.

That is why James 4:7 says, "Resist the devil and he shall flee." That is why Ephesians 4:27 says that we are to give no place to the devil. That is why the Bible says we are to have discernment. That is why Ephesians 1:22 says we are to put these things under our feet and become pure spiritually.

What does it mean to be pure spiritually? It means you are acting out according to the nature of God as He created you from the foundation of the world. That is spiritual purity. Spiritual impurity is you allowing the mentality and mind of Satan through his kingdom to operate through you, influence you, speak through you, act through you and do its dastardly deeds through you.

This is not just an emotion. Therapists are talking about inner healing, emotional healing and dealing with the emotions. I finally said to one of them, "You know, I hear this continual theme of emotions, emotional thought, emotional healing and dealing with our emotions." I said,

184

"Have you ever considered the fact that our emotions and our thoughts may not be emotional, but may be spiritual with an emotional expression?" There was silence. No, they had not considered the fact that rage is an evil spirit and not an emotion. These are Christian therapists. Well, you can manage your emotions all you want. But if you do not deal with the spirit that is behind it, you are in for a lifelong struggle with your inner man, because the evil is in your fallen inner man.

If you are not sure about that, you can go over to Mark 7:18-23 for an example. Jesus said, "That which comes out of the man is what defiles a man, not that which goes into the man in the form of food. For from within, out of the heart of man proceeds evil thoughts."

So evil thoughts, adulteries, fornications, murders, thefts, covetousness, wickedness, deceit, lasciviousness, an evil eye, blasphemy, pride, foolishness and all these evil things come from within and defile the man. Jesus said that which cometh out of the man, defileth the man. What is coming out of the man is what is within the heart of man; it expresses itself in a thought, a word or an action. A thought, a word or an action that is within the spiritual dynamics of the man will manifest and comes up in thought, word or deed. That is the expression of the evil spirit.

Do you know how many people do not realize that Fear is a sin? Fear is a sin because Fear says that evil is greater than the goodness of God. Fear says the worst that can happen to you will happen, and God is not able to lead you, He is not able to protect you, and He is not able to do anything.

But what does faith say? In Romans 14:23, even concerning the eating of food, it says, "Whatsoever is not of faith is sin." What is the opposite of faith? Fear. Fear is a sin

185

because God is not afraid of anything. Since you are created in His likeness and His image, why should you be afraid? If you are afraid of anything, you are under bondage.

Now there are things concerning wisdom of life that could be considered Fear. For example, there are godly elements of fear. When you are driving on the wrong side of the road and reading your Bible at the same time because you are so hungry for God's Word, then you look up and here comes a car about 100 paces down the road. Your heart jumps in your throat, the adrenaline starts to flow, and you yank the wheel. What struck you? That would be fear, but that is not an evil spirit of Fear; that is what God created you to do when dealing with the situations of life that would be dangerous to you. That is not sin.

The Fear that represents your future, the Fear that comes and keeps you from being that man or woman of God, is the type of Fear that is sin. Fear of rejection, Fear of failure, Fear of man, Fear of abandonment, Fear of flying, Fear of jumping, Fear of snoring, Fear of eating, Fear of this, Fear of that and all the different kinds of Fear — these are sins, so just call them sins. This is sin because it takes something away from you that does not need to be taken away.

A lot of people fly, but a lot of people do not fly because they are afraid. The only difference between people who fly and people who do not fly is Fear. Well, the plane may crash. Well, what if it did? Are you right with God? Go fly and have a good day. What is the worst thing that could happen to you? You would die and go to heaven.

The Bible says there are many voices, none without significance. What are these voices telling you and what is your heart telling you? Did God call you to go there or not? Are you wanting to go there out of your own spirit, out of your own heart, out of your own wanting to help someone? Or did God call you specifically to go to this place?

Psalm 37:23 says, "The steps of a righteous man are ordered of the Lord." Either your steps are ordered of the Lord, or you are being led by your own spirit. If God called you to go there, He is able to take you there and bring you back safely.

Sometimes if you go, there are persecutions. Maybe we always want to go somewhere and never have an obstacle. There is a popular mentality that God is with us only when things are going smoothly, and there are no obstacles. There is this mentality that Satan does not resist God's people and whatever they are doing. If you have a little resistance, you say I am not going. I have this little feeling, and I am not going to push through.

I do not find in the Bible where it says, for as many as are led by the words of others are the sons of God. I do not find in the Word where it says, those who are led by their feelings and their Fears are the sons of God. Romans 8:14 says, "For as many as are led by the Spirit of God are the sons of God." Are you led by the Spirit of God or are you led by the devil of Fear?

I have made some very scary decisions in my time, but I felt led by the Spirit. When I move in that dimension, there are not too many times I am wrong. Now how do you distinguish the difference? I can't teach that; it comes from within you because otherwise you would be following me. Being led by God is a learning experience, and sometimes not without its difficulty. I remember what Paul said to one of the churches. He had been trying to go there and exhort them. He said, "I would have come to you sooner, but Satan hindered me." What does he mean? That kingdom had hindered his forward motion. So if you are saying you are going to go somewhere or do something based on the absence of difficulty or conflict, then you do not understand the battleground. There is a very real battleground that would try to keep you from going where you need to go. I am spending so much time on this, because I want you to see the armor of the enemy.

In Luke 11, the "strong man armed" is the principality or evil spirit that lives in your palace. He lives in your palace and his goods are in place. Every bit of his kingdom that he is banking on to control you is in place and operating very well. For example, if you are dealing with the root of Bitterness, then all seven of these underlings (unforgiveness, resentment, rage, anger and wrath, hatred, violence, murder) are working to get control over you so that at least if you do not murder someone with a gun, you will do it with your tongue. When you murder someone with your tongue, all seven of these things are the goods that are in peace. These characters are very happy being alive in you and working through you.

The Unloving spirit has armor. It has goods that the strong man is trusting in. Self-Pity is part of its armor. Why is Self-Pity so dangerous? It promotes the kingdom of Self, not the kingdom of God. Has the kingdom of God come upon you, or has the kingdom of Self and self-preservation, self-idolatry, self-identification, self-introspection, self-hatred and self-rejection come upon you? Do you want the kingdom of God to be in you or do you want the kingdom of the devil? It is your choice. Being tormented is a way of life for some people, and they are content in it.

Anyway, when a strong man armed keepeth his palace… Can we finally deduce from this conversation that the palace is your house? So there is a strong man armed that is keeping your house, and his goods are in peace. Could we say that his goods will be the fruit of his labors? What would be the fruit of labor for Bitterness? Its fruit would be all seven of these to begin with – unforgiveness, resentment, retaliation, anger and wrath, hatred, violence, murder. "When someone stronger than the strong man shall come upon him and overcome him, he taketh from him all his armor wherein he trusted and divideth his spoils." That word "spoil" is a term of war. When you go in and overcome an enemy, you get all of his goods because that is the conquest of war.

Bitterness has seven areas that are very important to him: he loves these characters. It is his purpose for being and he is trusting that when you are dealing with that root of Bitterness, he is trusting with all of his might while sitting in your house, that resentment is as far as he is going to have to go. But over here wrath and anger are saying, "Wait a minute resentment, you're going to have to crank this thing up because I've got nothing to do. I'm in torment and the only way that I can get some peace is to manifest my nature." Bitterness, the strong man, says, "Yeah guys, let's pump this thing up. Let's set the scenario up that we can fulfill all of this in the person's life." This is the armor he is trusting in so he can keep his position in rulership, because he is sitting on the throne where you should be. He is enthroned in your castle, your house.

First Corinthians 6:19 says that you are the temple of the Holy Ghost. Are you the temple of devils? Are you a habitation of devils? When some of these things rise up and that person opens his mouth, you had better duck because he is throwing fiery darts. You think he missed you, but it comes right back and clumps you right in the back of the head, boom! Wait a minute. That's not fair. Fiery darts! We are dealing with a principality called an Unloving spirit, and it is trusting in the fact that it can control you with its armor, which is other spirits lesser than itself.

ARMOR TIED TO FEAR

There is another principality right beside it linked arm to arm with the Unloving spirit, and that is Fear. An Unloving spirit is deeply rooted in Fear. Fear is an antichrist spirit too. Second Timothy 1:7 says,

> **For God hath not given us the spirit of fear; but of power, and of love, and of a sound mind.**   2 Timothy 1:7

We proved that the Unloving spirit is an antichrist spirit. Fear is an antichrist spirit because it says that you have been given a spirit of Fear, and it is normal for you to be afraid. When you do not like yourself, you are afraid of yourself. So you have to accept yourself without Fear.

The devil created the Barbie Doll image, because it is a perverse image. There is not one female in the world that has ever been genetically created to match it. There is a spirit behind it that wants to control. As is the case of most matriarchal, witchcraft figurines, the man really does not count anyway. When you study matriarchal control, it always has offered itself as a beauty queen.

Matriarchal control portrays itself as a beauty queen.

First Peter 3:4 says a woman is not to be overly adorned. She is to look like the human being she was created to be. There is a spirit in the world that is built on lust and deception that tries to tell a woman that, in order to get a man, she has to look a certain way. Everything comes from the failure of men, but behind it is a spirit that controls. The women fall for it because they want to be accepted, and they want to be loved.

The failure of all of mankind is the man's responsibility. If the husbands would love their wives and the daddies would love their daughters, then they would not be competing. That scripture says it is the "inner man" that is the beautiful part of the woman. It is that inner part, that quiet and meek spirit.

It is the beauty of response to the correctness of love. Not creating it, but responding to it. God knew what He was doing. He made the females beautiful and soft and responsive and emotional. You ladies ought to be happy you are ladies, and the men ought to respect you and appreciate you and take care of you. Ephesians 5:28 says that a man who hates his wife, hates himself. Talk about some self-hatred. So the root of all abuse is self-hatred, which is an Unloving spirit.

Those who abuse, physically and verbally, and those who have a bully mentality, will attack if they find any person who has a weakness. If a bully can't find a victim he will create one, because he has to victimize. Some are programmed to abuse; some are programmed to reject. You may have been programmed to reject others because you yourself have been rejected. Just say the wrong thing, do the wrong thing, look at you the wrong way and that Rejection rises right up. That is armor. That strong man is banking on the fact that he can control you any way he wants to. If you think you have it all together today, he will find someone in your day that has that spirit too, and that spirit will be prompted to say and do something around you to trigger the one within you. Now we have spiritual ping-pong. You no longer have two people; you have two evil spirits loving every minute of their fulfillment. They are not in torment; they are happy.

Do you know that when rage and anger is roaring through you, it is as happy as it can be? Do you know when Rejection is flashing within you, it is as happy as it can be? Do you know those feelings of Unloving are right there chewing your ear off, and they are just as happy as they can be?

It is being fulfilled, it is acting out its nature, and it is having a field day. The Unloving spirit sitting on the throne of your life is saying, "Yeah, have a good day boys and girls. Go get 'em. Yeah, just tear them apart today."

That is the bottom line. If you do not understand that, you are lost in the shuffle. You need to have some discernment – get your eyes open, know what is not you, and deal with it! That is the armor. The armor of the Unloving spirit links with Fear.

SELF-REJECTION AND SELF-HATRED

Part of the armor that can be found around the Unloving spirit includes self-rejection. The first part of this word includes "self." What is self-rejection? Self-Rejection just accuses you to yourself. Self-Rejection and self-hatred are not the same thing. Self-Hatred wants you destroyed. There is a difference between you not accepting yourself and you wanting to destroy yourself. Self-Rejection will be rooted in self-fear. Actually self-rejection is more tied to Fear than you can imagine — you are afraid of yourself and rejecting yourself. Self-Rejection would be tied to Fear. In the case of diseases that come out of self-hatred, we have the autoimmune component.

Autoimmune Diseases

An autoimmune disease is one in which your body attacks itself biologically. That is classic in the spiritual understanding of roots to disease. As you attack yourself in self-hatred, your body will respond accordingly. In autoimmune diseases your white corpuscles, like your B cells and killer cells, and the marrow of your bone, are designed to attack the viruses and bacteria, and this is your immune system. God designed you with white corpuscles to attack invading bacteria.

A national statistic from the medical society is that the average person develops cancer cells at least 200 times in a lifetime. A healthy immune system will attack that mutated cell. It will recognize it as an invader, attack it and destroy it before it has a chance to get a foothold. The white corpuscles were created by God to attack invading organisms that could be harmful to you.

When you become harmful to yourself and reject yourself, this is an antichrist mentality. If you reject the fact that you belong on this planet, you reject God's love, and you won't love yourself. You not only have self-rejection, but you listen to it telling you it is a mistake that you are on this planet. You may as well be dead. You need to be eliminated, and you know everyone feels the same way. Then a spirit of infirmity comes into you.

Self-Rejection says you are a mistake.

The book of Proverbs says,

> As the bird by wandering, as the swallow by flying, so the curse causeless shall not come.   Proverbs 26:2

In the curses in Deuteronomy 28, it lists every disease known to man and then it says, "Other diseases not listed in this book shall be added unto you."

> [60]Moreover he will bring upon thee all the diseases of Egypt, which thou wast afraid of; and they shall cleave unto thee.

193

> [61]Also every sickness, and every plague, which is not
> written in the book of this law, them will the LORD bring
> upon thee, until thou be destroyed.   Deuteronomy 28:60-61

What causes the genetic code of the white corpuscle to be changed, so that it decides genetically that it is not the bacteria that is the enemy, but the enemy is the myelin sheath around your nerve or the connective tissue of your organs or the lining of your colon and on and on it goes? What do you think causes that white corpuscle to start attacking those various parts of your body? In our literature we have something called "white corpuscle deviant behavior."

Deviant Behavior

Deviant behavior is *behavior that is not normal*. Rage and anger are deviant types of behavior. Self-Hatred and Fear are deviant types of behavior. There are psychological therapy groups all over the world that have been raised up to help you deal with your deviant behavior and teach you how to live with it or help you identify with it. They call them archetypes and dark shadows.

Psychology and psychotherapy are to help you deal with your deviant thinking. Deviant thinking will produce deviant biological breakdown which is called disease.

The whole modality of care called allopathic medicine, which is traditional American medicine, is designed to try and meet deviant physiological breakdown which is called disease. What do you think produces that disease? They do not know. Etiology unknown! What does etiology unknown mean? Whenever I see "etiology unknown" in the Merck Manual, it is automatically a spiritual root. Whenever I see "viral," it automatically has a spiritual root. Whenever I hear the word "incurable," it automatically has a spiritual root.

194

So if by hating yourself there is a possibility that you could get an autoimmune disease, is that a high price to pay for that armor? Self-Hatred is armor that answers to the strong man, and that antichrist spirit that is called the Unloving spirit. An Unloving spirit is not given to you by God, but by the enemy, and you have agreed. You have agreed that this is part of your creation, and it is what is best for you. You are going to dress up in it and act out its nature every single day in your existence.

Crucifying the flesh is to crucify the old nature and the old man, which is the body of sin and the evil spirit reality that lives within you. When it says you are to die to self, die to the old man, you are to make these entities and the strong man no longer a part of your life. To do this, call them by name and say,

"You have to go. You're not part of my life. Go in the name of Jesus. I refuse to cohabit with you. You're not going to rule my house. I am the temple of the Holy Ghost. God has created me in my sovereignty. I am redeemed, and I am taking my life back. You cannot come along for the ride."

You have to take this position. There is a mentality in the church today that if you do not have it together spiritually, then you are inferior spiritually. That is incorrect because if you have arrived, then you need to do Galatians 6:1-2 and get down there in the mud to help others in their battles for their lives.

The Word says that he that would be greatest amongst you would be servant to all.

¹Brethren, if a man be overtaken in a fault, ye which are spiritual, restore such an one in the spirit of meekness; considering thyself, lest thou also be tempted.
²Bear ye one another's burdens, and so fulfil the law of Christ.   Galatians 6:1-2

195

An Unloving spirit will produce all autoimmune diseases. If you look in your family tree and find any autoimmune diseases, you need to wake up. This is the time to get it broken. You won't get it broken if you do not deal with the Unloving, unclean spirit that rules you and makes you not accept and love yourself. *This is critical to your health.*

The discerning of spirits is one of the nine gifts of the Holy Spirit. Open your heart for God to start working with you in what you need to discern in your own life. Why are you paying attention to the speck in your brother's eye when you do not deal with the beam in your own?

Self-Hatred can produce all autoimmune diseases. So can self-rejection. Do you recognize any of these in someone else's life? So you need to look in the mirror. "You old ugly looking thing you. You have the ugliest looking eyes I have ever seen." You fear your eyes, you fear your nose, and you fear who you are. You fear if you are smart enough, and you fear that you are going to fail. This is part of the armor, but it is now tied to Fear. It is difficult to go through the armor of the Unloving spirit and not tie Fear to it because Fear links with it side by side.

The Unloving spirit and Fear are linked side by side.

You can't defeat Fear if you do not start loving yourself in spite of it, because you are going to be exposed to Rejection by others. You are going to find someone who treats you as if you are not whole. Fear is going to be there demanding equal time in your life. It will be banging on your door trying to get you to listen to it. That is the way it is.

196

So when it comes banging on your door, if you have not dealt with the antichrist mentality that says you're not accepted of God, you're not loved, you don't belong here, then you will never defeat Fear. It attacks you personally most of the time. It projects possible failures in how you think and how you act, and it tells you that you don't look just right, or that your clothes aren't as nice as someone else's. It just constantly attacks self.

If you do not accept yourself, you can't defeat any other self-spirits. If you do not accept yourself unconditionally and get that antichrist, Unloving spirit out of you, you will never be able to totally defeat any of the self-spirits because they are there to reinforce themselves and explain to you why you are failing as a person in some dimension.

Competition

There is so much competition. What does competition tell you? You are not a whole person unless you win. "He that tries to save his own life shall lose it, and he that will lose his own life shall save it."

> **For whosoever will save his life shall lose it; but whosoever shall lose his life for my sake and the gospel's, the same shall save it.** Mark 8:35

Don't worry about who you are. Quit comparing yourself to others. Do you know what the Pharisees would do? They would see all these people who were not Pharisees, and they would pray this prayer to God: "Oh God, I thank you that I am not like these worms that I have to associate with. I thank you that the good work that you have done in my life is so complete that I do not have to associate with these undesirable spiritual ones." You are going to have to accept yourself right where you are.

Remember Luke 11 says, "The strong man armed keepeth his palace." That is self-enthronement. You are enshrined in yourself. All you think about is your realities and what's going on in your life. Me, me, me, self, self, self. If you want to be a candidate for greatness in the kingdom of God, quit trying to be anything because God is the one that selects. Even in the gifts of the Holy Spirit, 1 Corinthians 12 says that it is the Holy Spirit who decides who He uses in the gifts.

All it says is that you should desire the best gift, and in that desire we will see if God the Holy Spirit agrees. That is why it is so dangerous when so many people who want to have the gift of prophecy just go out and start doing it anyway. That is just them prophesying out of their spirit, or worse, it is an evil spirit of divination using them in their self-exaltation. If the Holy Spirit wants to use you in the gift of prophecy, you could not stop yourself if you tried because He is the one who decides. You are in fellowship with Him.

How does God think? Matthew says,

> [14]For *the kingdom of heaven is* as a man travelling into a far country, *who* called his own servants, and delivered unto them his goods.
> [15]And unto one he gave five talents, to another two, and to another one; to every man according to his several ability; and straightway took his journey.   Matthew 25:14-15

Did it mean that the person who got five talents was any more important than the one that got two or the one that got one? No, the Lord gave it according to the ability. Did it mean that the person who got one was less trusted than the one that got five? No. You will find out the one with one had a real problem – Fear.

The talents were given according to the ability God created in him to use them, because when you read this further, they multiply. The ones who received five, gained five more, and the one that received two, gained two more. But the one that received only one talent, he did not multiply it; he went and hid it. He buried it because he was afraid that his master would be mad at him if he lost it, so he hung onto it and he buried it. When the master came, he called him an unfaithful servant because the least he could have done was to give the goods to interest, but he did not even do that. He hid it in Fear.

This example is dealing with competition, with self-rejection, and with people who are comparing themselves to others. Comparing yourself to another is competition and is part of the Unloving spirit. If we are comparing ourselves to others, we are not comparing ourselves to God. We want His sovereignty in our life, yet we are subjecting ourselves to others' approval and worth as we perceive it.

When we compare ourselves to others or compete with others, *we are not accepting who we are and what God has given us.* Many people say, "Well, I'm not going to do anything. I'm no one. I can't speak." You talk about a guy with an Unloving spirit! That was Moses. He was called the meekest man that ever lived, but at the same time he had such Fear of speaking that he told God he could not even speak for Him because he had Fear. God said that Aaron would be his spokesman, so when Moses had something to say, Aaron said it. That is not what God intended. It was to Moses' shame, because God accommodated him in his self-rejection.

Comparison to others
is the work of the Unloving spirit.

God is sovereign in giving talent. If a person seems to be more able or is doing more for God than you are, does that mean you are a lesser person? No, but an Unloving spirit will tell you that you don't measure up. It will say, "Well,

199

I'm no one unless I have five talents." Well, if one talent is what you have, that is the ability God has given you. That is what He has called you to do, so do it!

You must accept yourself and stand against the armor that says you don't measure up. If God puts you in this church to do something, and you say to me, "Well, someone else more important than I am should be doing this," then what are you saying? You are saying, first of all, that I made a mistake, and I do not know what I am doing. Number two, you are saying that you have self-rejection and an Unloving spirit.

If I wanted that other person to do it, guess who would be doing it. They would, because I am picking out people according to the ability I feel God has placed within them. If I did not feel that, I would not use them. They may not have grown into it yet. If you want to be an astronaut, you do not just jump on the space shuttle and fly away. Do you think astronauts who fly in space are chosen on the basis of having it all together? They are chosen by someone who says they have the ability to grow into it. Then what do they do? They do simulations and practices. They master their math and their trigonometry and everything else they have learned. When they were selected, they did not jump into a space capsule and fly away. When I get involved with people, I have to be sensitive to what God has called them to do.

I am talking about determining your value. When you start looking at the part of you that is not what God created, what are you going to have left? What are you going to do with your day if you do not have self-hatred to think about? What are you going to do with your day if you do not spend half of it dealing with Fear?

What in the world would you do with yourself if you did not have this stuff that is not part of your life? How much time do we spend a day on things that are really not what God created? A lot! Now there are certain necessary parts of life that seem to be mundane and losses of time, but that is life. We are not talking about those things. We are talking about the parts of you that are not really you.

Selfishness

Selfishness is another one that is not you. That is a big one. Isaiah talks about Lucifer:

> ¹²**How art thou fallen from heaven, O Lucifer, son of the morning! *how* art thou cut down to the ground, which didst weaken the nations!**
> ¹³**For thou hast said in thine heart, I will ascend into heaven, I will exalt my throne above the stars of God: I will sit also upon the mount of the congregation, in the sides of the north:** Isaiah 14:12-13

Here is the beginning of selfishness. "…you have said in your heart, I…" Do you see the big "I" there? Lucifer was placed to serve God in the rulership of the beings that were here on this planet before the Ice Age. Those beings fell with one-third of all angels, and Lucifer led them in rebellion against God. The beginning of introspection, looking inward to the kingdom of Self, begins with the word "I."

Luke 22:26 says that he who would be greatest among you is he that would be least. He that would be greatest among you is he that would serve.

Matthew 23:11 says he that would be greatest among you is he that would be servant of all.

Now when you are servant of all, are you looking inward or outward? There has to come in time when you submit yourself to the sovereign God. There has to come a place when you line up with God and His creation. You need to understand what is meant to be the mirror image of the living God. Jesus came as the express image, the mirror image of the living God.

> Who being the brightness of *his* glory, and the express image of his person, and upholding all things by the word of his power, when he had by himself purged our sins, sat down on the right hand of the Majesty on high; Hebrews 1:3

When Jesus came and died for you, He had that moment when He said, "If it be possible..." He dipped into self and said, "If it be possible, Father, take this cup from me." It was the cup of bitterness, the cup of death. "If it be possible, take this cup" and then instantly He said, "Nevertheless, not My will but Thy will be done."

> And he went a little farther, and fell on his face, and prayed, saying, O my Father, if it be possible, let this cup pass from me: nevertheless not as I will, but as thou *wilt*.
> Matthew 26:39

What did Jesus do? He came from introspection at the point of the crucifixion and looked outward as servant of all. He did not get caught in Self-Pity. He did not have an Unloving spirit. The Bible says He was rejected even of God, and that God turned His face from Him.

> And about the ninth hour Jesus cried with a loud voice, saying, Eli, Eli, lama sabachthani? that is to say, My God, my God, why hast thou forsaken me? Matthew 27:46

Do you think that would be Rejection? From the human standpoint you probably could consider it being rejected by God, but did God reject Him? No, He raised Him from the dead. Romans says,

> That if thou shalt confess with thy mouth the Lord Jesus, and shalt believe in thine heart that God hath raised him from the dead, thou shalt be saved. Romans 10:9

202

If you believe in your heart that God the Father raised Christ Jesus from the dead, you shall be saved.

Matthew 14:36 says that in the garden of Gethsemane Jesus looked outward and He said, "Nevertheless, not My will be done."

"I" and "I will" are all part of the armor of an Unloving spirit. An antichrist spirit will always protect itself, develop itself and look into itself. A spirit that is not antichrist will look past itself and look at the overall picture around it. Part of your success in gaining freedom from an Unloving spirit is, first of all, to look out of yourself. Look at those around you who have rejected you or made you victims, and realize they had these problems.

You have to see who you are becoming. You have to be able to see it in your heart. If you can't see it, you are not going there. Hebrews 11:1 says faith is the substance of things hoped for. What are you hoping for? A different way of thinking? A different nature? You can't have a different way of thinking if you are not spiritually changed on the inside. It's not possible. Proverbs 23:7 says, "As a man thinketh in his heart, so is he."

Isaiah says,

> 13For thou hast said in thine heart, I will ascend into heaven, I will exalt my throne above the stars of God: I will sit also upon the mount of the congregation, in the sides of the north:
> 14I will ascend above the heights of the clouds; I will be like the most High. Isaiah 14:13-14

I will, I will. The nature of Satan is that of self-exaltation. An Unloving spirit will always exalt itself. Have you ever seen anyone that was dressed up in despair? Have you ever seen anyone that had Self-Pity? Did you see how it is a state of being?

203

Attention Getting

A person who has an Unloving spirit also will want attention Part of the armor is an attention getting spirit. Let me give you an example. A bully has a spirit of Rejection and an Unloving spirit. He compensates for that by bravado to get attention in order to cover up his spiritual deficiencies.

Excessive Talkativeness

Another piece of armor that is designed to hide the strong man of the Unloving spirit is excessive talkativeness. When you will see someone who always has something to say, nonstop, that person has deeply rooted insecurity, which is Fear.

Remember that the Unloving spirit is a principality, an antichrist spirit, and links arms with another principality called Fear.

You cannot defeat Fear
unless you have defeated the Unloving spirit.

First John 4:18 says "perfect love casts out Fear." So how are you going to defeat Fear? Perfect love. It begins by receiving the love of the Godhead, loving yourself and loving others. When you have mastered these three areas of your life, Fear does not stand a chance. If you want to defeat this principality at the level he operates, then face him and…

Accept yourself, unconditionally.

Be prepared to deal with the armor of the Unloving spirit. It does not matter who puts you down. There is a requirement and responsibility on your part to act godly. This is all predicated on one axiom of truth: that you are godly too. You are going to have to be a man or woman of God. If you are not prepared to be godly, you are not prepared to stand in the world as light and salt. Matthew 5:13 says you are to be the light of the world and the salt of the earth. You give it flavor. *Someone has to get spiritual first.* Jesus died to make it possible for you to be a man or woman of God. That is what we need in the earth. We do not need perfect people. We just need people who take responsibility. There is nothing more edifying than to see a leader take responsibility for a mistake. It is an example to the people. It is a tremendous thing when a leader says, "I just blew it. I am sorry. I take full responsibility for that." They may lynch him because everyone wants others to be perfect, without being perfect themselves! If we would have more grace and mercy for the leaders of our government, they might confess more. Then we would not have to have special councils raised up to make them confess.

Self-Exaltation

Lucifer said, "I will. I will." Not only did Lucifer rise up against God, but he tempted one-third of all angels to sin with him. They said, "I will. I will." Lucifer tempted the angels with self-exaltation. When he took the serpent as a medium of expression after he fell, and he was in the earth invisible as Satan, what did he tempt Eve with? He said, "You shall be as gods."

Genesis 3:5 says,

> **For God doth know that in the day ye eat thereof, then your eyes shall be opened, and ye shall be as gods, knowing good and evil.** Genesis 3:5

Satan didn't tell Eve those "gods" were evil spirits who knew good and evil.

If you study mythology, there are gods. Every mythological figure has a part of its nature that is fallen, even to incest, to murder, to rape and to strife. It begins when Uranus killed his father Cronus and took over the kingdom of earth. Right up front is anarchy against a father. Who raised his ugly head against the Father of all spirits?

205

Lucifer. That becomes the foundation for all mythology, to overthrow the father. The plan of Satan in your life is to overthrow the Father's will.

What did Jesus say? "Not My will be done, Father, but Thy will be done." What did Jesus say in the Lord's prayer? The disciples said, "Teach us to pray." Jesus said, "Our Father...Thy will be done." Part of the armor of an Unloving spirit is a fabricated self, which is not the extension of what God created. It is what you have created for yourself. People who have an Unloving spirit try to create a niche for themselves that is fabricated, rather than growing naturally with God leading by the Spirit and becoming what God wants them to be. They had to create something to hide the insecurity, to hide the Unloving spirit.

Look at the situation with Marilyn Monroe. She created an illusion to hide the fact that she hated herself and was tormented. She had an Unloving spirit. She had everything and she covered it, but she did not cover it well. I will. I, I, I...

Self-Mutilation

Another fruit of the Unloving spirit is self-mutilation. This is one of the fastest growing realities of young teenage girls in America, from piercing and scarring and everything else. Bulimia and anorexia are rooted in self-mutilation.

How does the devil do this? When you have an Unloving spirit that has attached itself to you, it tells you that you are not the nicest thing God ever created. If you listen to this long-term, that spirit becomes part of your life.

One of the first things that happens to the endocrine system is a reduction in the secretion of serotonin. When you have a decreased serotonin level, you do not like yourself, and as long as you do not like yourself, it will stay there. The only way to remove it is to give a drug-induced, artificial reality to boost it or to circumvent it.

Fen-Phen and other diet drugs were designed to elevate or boost serotonin levels. When your serotonin levels are up, you feel good about yourself. This is how easy it is to get you. Your enemy knows you. He knows everything about you physiologically. He knows everything about the mind-body connection, and he knows everything about your chemistry.

You need to know him. That's what discernment is – knowing your enemy. It is a finely developed tool because without discernment you are blind. If you do not have discernment, you're lost in the shuffle. The Unloving spirit triggers the underproduction of serotonin, and that feeling of unloveliness is now reinforced. Now it is not just reinforced by a spirit projecting those thoughts into your consciousness or through your spirit. It's reinforced by a chemical imbalance that produces a physiological response as well as an emotional and spiritual one. Now you have a problem.

Excessive Eating

Drugs such as Fen-Phen were designed to boost serotonin levels. If you feel good about yourself, you do not eat as much. A fruit of the armor for an Unloving spirit is excessive eating – bingeing. The loss of serotonin in your body, as your pineal gland responds to this conflict in the soul, is a by-product, but it produces a cause and effect. Now we have an understanding as to how this is working.

When you come into self-rejection, it reinforces self. It tells you that you are not a whole person; it tells you that you are a non-person. All victimization comes out of people hating themselves, and if you hate yourself, you are going to hate your neighbor.

207

If you hate yourself, you also hate your neighbor.

Lucifer was part of heaven. He was an archangel. The angels that fell with Lucifer became part of the body of Satan. Are you part of a body? Are you part of the body of Christ?

> ¹²For as the body is one, and hath many members, and all the members of that one body, being many, are one body: so also *is* Christ.
> ¹³For by one Spirit are we all baptized into one body, whether we be Jews or Gentiles, whether we be bond or free; and have been all made to drink into one Spirit.
> ¹⁴For the body is not one member, but many.
>
> 1 Corinthians 12:12-14

In the parable of the talents, the lord of this group of servants knew each individual personally. He had to because he said he gave to one, five and to one, two and to one, one, according to their individual abilities. He did not give everything to the one who could handle five did he? He did not say to the one that he gave five, "You know your ability is greater than the servant to whom I'm going to give one talent. So I'm going to let you handle all of my responsibilities, because you are the best one I have."

No, he took each of them and he gave to them five and two and one, according to their ability. For the one that received one talent, did the lord consider that person valuable? Did he consider that person part of the picture? Was the responsibility placed on the shoulder of the person who got one talent, the same as the responsibility placed on the one he gave five? When you read the conclusion of the parable, the answer is yes. Did it make the person who only got one talent inferior or less of a person than the one that got five? Not at all.

Self-Idolatry, Idolatry, Self-Comparison

You can't compare yourself to another. An Unloving spirit will have something called self-comparison. What is wrong with self-comparison? Everything! It makes the person you are comparing yourself to like a god to you, and that is idolatry. So the armor includes self-idolatry and idolatry of others. Self-Comparison is a spiritual action, a spiritual root.

Have you ever noticed people who are good looking? When they have self-rejection and an Unloving spirit, they will always find someone to hang out with that doesn't look quite as good as they do because they can't stand to be compared with someone who, in their eyes, looks better than they do. The choice of friends is coming out of self-rejection and an Unloving spirit, not because that was a true friend that God planned and wanted for them. It was because they felt more comfortable with someone who was not in competition with them.

In the business world, you have heard that it is good to hang out with successful people. That is what networking is about. Why are you hanging out with successful people? It is because you feel inferior from the standpoint of who you are in that particular arena. If you are not careful you will become an extension of that person. It is possible for God to make you more successful than the one you are using as a standard. If you use another person as your god or your standard of who you should be, you are now becoming an extension of *his* image, not God's image. You need to be really careful that you do not pattern yourself after humanistic ways of success. You need to be very careful that you do not consider human success to be a godly reality. There is nothing wrong with success, but when you become preoccupied with success and perfectionism, it leads you to idolatry.

209

Perfectionism, Self-Accusation, Self-Condemnation

Under the Unloving spirit of this idolatry, there is another piece of armor called perfectionism. Perfectionism does not allow for failure. An Unloving spirit does not allow you to fail, and when you do, it produces self-accusation and self-condemnation.

These are all spirits. These are the goods right here. This is the strong man armed keeping his palace. In every person who is struggling with an Unloving spirit, you will find many of these areas as part of his spiritual and psychological battle. When that thought comes up, you say, "Wait a minute you are some of those goods. That strong man is trusting in the fact that you are going to keep me from being free. I want to identify you right now; you are not me." These are perfectionism, self-accusation and self-condemnation.

Self-Bitterness

Self-Bitterness also comes out of an Unloving spirit. Self-Bitterness will produce unforgiveness towards self. That is armor for an Unloving spirit. It is always concerned about self, self, self. Self-Unforgiveness is unforgiveness towards self. In ministry, I ask people to say, "I forgive myself," and many get lockjaw instantly. We must learn to forgive ourselves.

Self-Resentment

Then there is self-resentment. "I can never do anything right. The harder I try, the behinder I get. I never have been any good, and never will be any good. I am just a nobody." That is coming out of self-resentment. "I ain't nobody. I remember Daddy told me that. Daddy knows best." Self-Resentment.

"I just do not like the way I look." There is a difference between Bitterness and Rejection. Self-Resentment is coming out of self-bitterness. Self-Rejection is coming out of Fear and is fed by Fear of self. The two antichrist spirits that are here, the Unloving spirit and Fear, stand side-by-side. It is all intertwined. So this is the armor.

So how do you spoil the goods? You identify each "good," each fruit of Satan's possession of your life and control of your life, and you start unraveling it. If you could not cut a rope, how do you think you could get it apart? Unravel it a strand at a time.

Unravel a strand at a time.

If you can't break it, you can cut a strand at a time. You may not have the force to cut the rope, but a rope is built up of several strands. It is not standing by itself. It can be torn apart.

Self-Retaliation

After self-bitterness, and self-resentment, there is self-retaliation. What would that include? Some of this is excessive eating and self-mutilation. When you have an Unloving spirit, and you have the root of self-bitterness and self-retaliation, they will cause you to go right into the face of someone you know is going to reject you. You go into it with your eyes wide open because you have a need to be rejected. Then the Unloving spirit comes up and starts accusing you and telling you that you are not loved; that is what produces continual victimization.

That is what drives a woman back to a husband who is beating her. You will find that a woman who is being beaten has a need to be beaten to reinforce that hatred of herself. She is a victim. She needs the mutilation. She needs that brutality. Actually *she* does not, but the Unloving spirit that

211

is in her will drive her right into the face of something that she knows that person is going to do.

Then she is going to be a victim all over again. The spirit within her is so strong it takes her right back into it, and she is unable to stop it. That is why they have battered women's shelters. It is time out, and time to get away from the abuser. Then you have to go back and say, "Well are you going to stay in this abusive pattern?"

There are, statistically, very few battered spouses that walk away from the situation because they do not understand their spiritual problems. They go back into it. When they go back into it, it is a freewill decision. They are trapped, and in that entrapment, there is a form of victimization that is rooted in an Unloving spirit. If you study these case histories, in most cases you will find that her mother was beaten by her husband, so it is also a generational pattern. When we find abuse, it is generational; this is an inherited thing that comes down through the family tree. The man that is abusing was abused himself; it is a pattern.

An Unloving spirit is tied directly to Fear, and Fear is a type of control. In some of the nations that are in human rights violations, the government is controlling the people through the fear of violent reprisal. That is a type of control rooted in Fear. When you get into victimization, that is a type of control, but behind the victimization is an Unloving spirit filled with self-hatred and self-rejection.

What is unfortunate within the programs that are available today in psychology and psychiatry and even in battered women's shelters is that they do not understand the spiritual dynamics. All they can say to the woman is, "We are going to protect you, and we suggest that you get counseling." The counseling is going to produce nothing,

212

because the man has an Unloving spirit. Not only does she have self-bitterness in the spousal abuse, but he does too.

When people get into self-bitterness, they have rage, anger, hatred, violence and murder. When they have self-retaliation, there is a force within them that takes over, and they are unable to stop. The only way to deal with it is for them to remove themselves totally from the situation.

So here is the next problem: when they have removed themselves totally, their next relationship has those same spirits. They still have the same spirits and do not know it, and all of a sudden they are into it again. The next relationship is as abusive as the first relationship. In the case of fathers who abuse their daughters, guess who the daughter usually marries. How many females have said, "The greatest tragedy of my life is that I tried to get away from my abusive father, and I married someone just like him."

When it comes to victimization, a good 90 percent of the time you will hear, "I married my father. I married what I hated in him." They do not know it until after the marriage. While they are dating, if a man shows any evidence of abuse either verbal or physical, they are in trouble because when they get married then they have the whole package.

Statistically, you will see patterns of victimization, good intentions and untrue statements from the person that he has changed. Now there are some people who make quality decisions, but statistically it is not very good. They need God; they need ministry and deliverance. What has them? Is it just an emotion? No, it is an Unloving spirit that is controlling them. How do we know it would be an antichrist spirit? It is because a man who hates himself does not take care of his wife when they become one flesh. This is self-bitterness.

Ephesians says,

> So ought men to love their wives as their own bodies. He that loveth his wife loveth himself. Ephesians 5:28

Now, what happens if you are already in an abusive relationship?

An abusive relationship reinforces your Unloving spirit.

It is going to reinforce the Unloving spirits in you. If at all possible, live peaceably one with another. When there is abuse between a husband and a wife, many pastors counsel immediate separation for the safety of the children and the wife, and to clear the air. How do you defeat an Unloving spirit? Get right with God. The first thing you do is reconcile with God to receive His love.

If you are not going to live together as one flesh in peace you had better separate, because James 3:16 says where there is strife, there is every evil thing. If you have an Unloving spirit and all of these things that are part of the armor, including self-bitterness, within you, there are also spirits within you that will pick a fight with someone. Have you ever been responsible for engineering strife? Has anything ever overtaken you, such that whatever another person said or did, it was not good enough? Have you ever seen anyone deliberately take a peaceful situation and insert a little chaos?

When a person has an Unloving spirit, it will engineer circumstances through the armor to get its fix so that it can manifest and run its course until the dastardly deed and damage have been done. When that is done and the air clears, everyone is back picking up the pieces again. "I'm sorry. I repent. I do not know what came over me. I do not know what got into me. I just couldn't stop it. Well that is

214

not really me." Do these words sound familiar? "Well, if you do it again, I am going to eat your lunch. You'd better watch out. Do not mess with me." An Unloving spirit will engineer circumstances to make sure the person is a victim.

The Unloving spirit engineers circumstances to victimize you.

Many times that person is an unwilling victim, but sometimes he (or she) is a willing victim. That is all rooted in self-bitterness and self-retaliation. A person who has an Unloving spirit will pick fights, just to get rejected. It will pick a fight and when the person gets a black eye, it will go around and say, "Look at this black eye. Look what they did to me." What is that speaking? Unforgiveness! Bitterness! I think there are certain people who get up in the morning so influenced by the second heaven that they look to pick a fight all day somewhere until it happens. Somewhere along the day, there is going to be a problem. People who have Unloving spirits go in and split churches, split families and ruin businesses. They're just looking for trouble. What is behind that? It is a root of Bitterness coming out of an Unloving spirit.

Romans says,

> If it be possible...live peaceably with all men.
>
> Romans 12:18

Self-Anger

How about self-anger? Have you ever experienced self-anger? Have you ever said I just can't stand myself? Have you ever been mad at yourself? That comes out of an Unloving spirit, perfectionism, self-accusation and self-condemnation. That will trigger, boom, boom, boom, right into self-anger. Self-Accusation and self-condemnation will trigger self-anger just like that. When that self-anger rises up, you had better keep your distance from it because you are going where angels fear to tread. When that self-anger rises up, it is no respecter of persons. If you are not careful, you are going to do something to yourself or someone else. The fruit of this is to make someone else a victim. The devil is no respecter of persons. He is an equal opportunity oppressor.

Self-Hatred

How about self-hatred? You do not go all the way to self-hatred unless you have the root of Bitterness against yourself, and you have come through all of these stages at some point. Self-Hatred is a progressive state. Self-Hatred is an advanced state of something that is simmering behind the scenes for days and weeks and months and years.

Self-Violence, Self-Torment

How about self-violence? There are people who get mad and hit themselves. If you are not delivered of this, you will duplicate it, and if you do not duplicate it, you will be tormented in it. You do not actually have to do this stuff, but you will be tormented with the forces that are accusing you of the possibility. Some people are tormented by fantasy projection of doing the evil they are capable of. It is accomplishing the same thing — self-torment. So remember that torment is a Fear issue.

If you have been a victim of anyone with an Unloving spirit, there has been an immediate transfer of those spirits into you, and they first come in the area of Fear. Insecurity is a Fear that is rooted in an Unloving spirit, but it is more Fear than Unloving. Everything you have been exposed to is capable of influencing you and becoming part of you.

In 1 John 4:18 it says that there is no Fear in love; perfect love casts out Fear. Fear hath torment. He that hath Fear is not made perfect in love. Here you see the close relationship between love and fear, and you will also see the close relationship between being unloved and being fearful. Right there you see these two principalities of Unloving and Fear, standing side-by-side.

One of the secrets to unraveling racial tension is loving each other. It is not through social programs or education. It is going down there in these communities and walking up to these people and telling them you love them and asking how you can serve them. It is not giving them social education programs and telling them to stay on the other side of the street. Perfect love casts out Fear — Fear of man, Fear of rejection, Fear of failure, Fear of abandonment, Accusation, condemnation. When you say you love God and hate your neighbor or your brother, the love of God is not within you. So we have to get our definitions straight here in order to defeat the Unloving spirit.

Do you have to do reality checks in your life when you have been around people who have rejected you? Does the Unloving spirit try to get hold of you with Rejection and Fear of Rejection? Is it trying to diminish who you are in your creation? Yes, it always is! It is like someone who has a disease. There is a stigma that comes with disease. It says that because you have a disease, you are not a whole person. Wait a minute. You can have a disease and be totally correct spiritually. Paul had a thorn in the flesh, and he was totally correct spiritually. Was he less of a person?

It is amazing those people point at others who have some kind of problem, whether psychological or biological or spiritual in their life, but they won't look at their own spiritual problems. Well this is mankind. But do you have to be a victim of mankind? Do you have to be a victim of others people's Unloving spirits?

One of the key things we say to people, at some point in ministry, is this: we want you to be able to be exposed to every evil reality in any living person and not be personally affected by it whatsoever. Wouldn't that be a great freedom for you to be exposed to all the evil in any human being and not take it in personally and not let it become part of your life? That would be a victory! Are we able to be free of an Unloving spirit and not be victimized again?

First John 4:18 part 4 says, "He that feareth is not made perfect in love." If you have an Unloving spirit in you, it is not possible for you to give and receive love properly, without Fear. He that feareth does so because of the breakdown in love. First John says,

> There is no fear in love; but perfect love casteth out fear: because fear hath torment. He that feareth is not made perfect in love.   1 John 4:18

If you have this kind of Unloving spirit, it is impossible for you to give and receive love without Fear.

Would you like to be able to give and receive love without Fear? Would you like to be able to give love, and it never be returned to you, and have that never affect you? If you are looking for something in return, there may be something in you needing to be loved. Who is your source? God or a person? You need to be so objective in receiving the love of God that if anyone smiles at you today, it is just a bonus. That is the completeness of the love of God that needs to come.

Would you like to hold out for a better life? Or do you just want to go to the halfway house? Many of us are living in a halfway house and call it freedom. God intended that we be spiritually free men and women. Do you know what the leavened gospel is? It says you can live in Egypt under

Pharaoh, and it is called freedom. Or you can live under Nebuchadnezzar, and that is called freedom. Or you live under the authority of someone else spiritually, and it is a form of freedom.

God's people went into captivity under Syria and Egypt and Mesopotamia and all those nations, but God delivered them from that type of bondage because it was spiritual oppression. Physical, emotional and spiritual oppression. In the Old Testament is the true test of freedom for God's people: when they lived in Israel with their capital city Jerusalem and they were free of war and oppression. That was the total proof of their freedom: when they lived with their husbands and wives and their children, had freedom from war and worshipped their God in total freedom. That is the kind of freedom God planned.

In the millennium the people shall live in unwalled cities with no more defenses and no more war. When you can live without a mechanism of protection from people who have Unloving spirits and want to make you a victim in their spiritual realities, that is freedom.

Would you like to be a free man or a free woman? Cohabitation with the enemy is not the true gospel. However, being free to serve God, being free to have your peace with yourself and with God and with others, now that is freedom. Some do not want to be free. Do you? Are you able to handle the fiery darts of unloveliness from other people and not be affected by them? I did not say you would not be defiled, but you don't have to take it in and repay evil with evil.

Defending Oneself

If we are not careful and do not deal with the Unloving spirit within us, then when other people have the same thing that is within us, that we are just suppressing, and they

219

come and get us, guess what is going to bubble to the surface. What does it want to do? Do the same thing to someone else that was just done to it. Did you ever notice when we are dealing with Rejection and Unloving spirits, that the stuff that bubbles up in you wants to do to others the same that has been done to you? But that is an antichrist mentality.

The Word says that we are to repay evil with good. If you have an Unloving spirit, you can't repay evil with good because Bitterness is there. Envy and Jealousy is there. Rejection is there. The Unloving spirit is there. Fear is there, and now you are back in the kingdom of Self. Self is always defending itself. Defending oneself is part of the armor. Defending oneself is coming out of Fear of Rejection. Defending oneself is rooted in Fear, but it is also tied directly to the Unloving spirit. You desperately need to feel safe. An Unloving spirit won't let you feel safe; it is tied to Fear.

When you are trying to make peace with people, and they become more and more angry, they have a root of Bitterness. You are casting your pearls before the swine. A little insight about Jesus is this: when they were ready to kill him, like when He was preaching and they wanted to stone Him, or when He went to His hometown and they wanted to throw Him over the cliff, He did not allow it to influence Him. He would vamoose. He would pass through them and disappear. He did not stand there and call down fire from heaven. He did not debate with them. He did not say they were wrong because they were not interested in peace. When you run across people who are not interested in peace, get away from them. If someone does not receive the gospel in peace, you need to terminate it and say, "I can see that we're not going to go anywhere. Let's just take time out, and we'll talk some other time." Get out of it! Pass through them. Get away. Get gone. Get out of it!

Matthew says,

> 7And as ye go, preach, saying, The kingdom of heaven is at hand.
>
> 8Heal the sick, cleanse the lepers, raise the dead, cast out devils: freely ye have received, freely give.
>
> 9Provide neither gold, nor silver, nor brass in your purses,
>
> 10Nor scrip for your journey, neither two coats, neither shoes, nor yet staves: for the workman is worthy of his meat.
>
> 11And into whatsoever city or town ye shall enter, enquire who in it is worthy; and there abide till ye go thence.
>
> 12And when ye come into an house, salute it.
>
> 13And if the house be worthy, let your peace come upon it: but if it be not worthy, let your peace return to you.
>
> 14And whosoever shall not receive you, nor hear your words, when ye depart out of that house or city, shake off the dust of your feet.
>
> 15Verily I say unto you, It shall be more tolerable for the land of Sodom and Gomorrha in the day of judgment, than for that city.　　　　　　　　　　　　　Matthew 10:7-15

This has to do with the preaching of the gospel, but in it is a seed of wisdom. The seed of wisdom is this, if you are coming bearing gifts of peace, which is what the gospel says to do, and you are coming with reconciliation and good things in your heart, if the people are evil then they won't receive it. Get away from it. If you can't leave your peace, shake the dust off your feet, and walk away from it. In the day of judgment, if it is not resolved it shall go worse for them than it did for the city of Sodom and Gomorrha, because you came with a right spirit. You came with gifts in your heart. You came trying to make reconciliation. You came with the gospel, but they were not interested in peace or reconciliation.

Don't get mad, call down fire from heaven to consume it in a moment and say, "God help you." Most people do not say that; most people say go to you-know-where and for God to do this to them and that to them. That is the first response coming out of Rejection if you do not have a right spirit. First you tell people to go to hell, and then you ask God to damn them. The first statement that comes out of an Unloving spirit is profanity. Profanity and the Unloving spirit go hand-in-hand.

There is an element of an Unloving spirit that will take people into a situation that needs to be fixed so they can feel good about themselves. There is an area in an Unloving spirit that can drive them to try to get something fixed so it can prove to them they are okay. They need to really guard their heart and understand why they have a need to make peace with them. The biggest reason is that the Lord says so, that we make peace with our brother. But what if they are not ready to receive you?

The Bible says not to reprove a scorner, because he is going to eat you for lunch. There are people you can't reason with, and they are not interested in reasoning with you. They are division-makers. They are not interested in peace. So what does the Bible say about those individuals? Mark them. Have nothing to do with them. Keep your distance from a person who is a habitual troublemaker and not interested in peace.

Need for Approval

The need for approval is armor. You can say, "I am so sad because I can't make peace with those people. They don't know how I have changed. I have really changed, and they won't even give me the time of day to share with them how I have changed." You have these people who are not interested in making peace with you, and if you are not careful a need for approval can come. What you are really saying in your heart is, "If they could see the changed person I am, then they would love me." Now the Word says they should love you from the beginning.

Galatians says,

> ¹Brethren, if a man be overtaken in a fault, ye which are spiritual, restore such an one in the spirit of meekness; considering thyself, lest thou also be tempted.
>
> ²Bear ye one another's burdens, and so fulfil the law of Christ.
> Galatians 6:1-2

So if they have eliminated you because you were at fault, if they were truly spiritual, they would forgive you, restore you and accept you. When someone blows something with you, your job is to come along beside them and help them identify the problem so they can recover themselves.

First Timothy says,

> ²⁴And the servant of the Lord must not strive; but be gentle unto all *men*, apt to teach, patient,
>
> ²⁵In meekness instructing those that oppose themselves; if God peradventure will give them repentance to the acknowledging of the truth;
>
> ²⁶And *that* they may recover themselves out of the snare of the devil, who are taken captive by him at his will.
> 2 Timothy 2:24-26

So you do not have someone operating with a full deck spiritually to begin with, but you are expecting them to be spiritual. You really have to understand something. You may know the truth of spiritual things and you may know what freedom is like, but that person may not. You can't ask an unrenewed, unregenerated person who does not know the Word of God and does not have the Spirit of God within them to do correct spiritual things. They probably have an Unloving spirit. They have Fear. They have Envy and Jealousy. They have Rejection. They have hatred. They have Bitterness, and they are going to act it out. The best thing you can do is keep your distance. Matthew 10:13-14 says if you can't leave your peace, do not go there.

Within all of us is a desire to make peace with other people. We want to be peacemakers. That is our heart. There is nothing wrong about wanting to be at peace with someone you are at odds with. That is scriptural. The Spirit of God would be there to assist you in that endeavor, but you have to be careful that the other person wants the same thing. It is a risk to ask someone to forgive you when that person is capable of eating you for lunch, but it is a risk worth taking. If that person rejects you and calls fire from heaven down on you, get away from him (or her). Do not be a victim. Your approval is not from a man. First Corinthians 2:15 says that no man is to judge us, only God who called us. No man has judged me or can judge me. If you are following the Word of God and you have a right spirit, then only God is your judge.

First Corinthians says,

> **For the body is not one member, but many.**
>
> 1 Corinthians 12:14

If the foot shall say, because I am not the hand, then I am not part of the body. Is it therefore not of the body? If the ears shall say because I am not the eye, I am not of the body. Is it therefore not of the body? If the whole body were an eye, then how could you hear? If the whole body were an ear that could hear, then how would you smell? But now, hath God the Father has set the members, every one of them, in the body as it hath pleased Him.

Actually God has a little mercy on some of you, because you are not spiritual; look at all the work you would have to do. To whom much has been given, much is required.

> **But he that knew not, and did commit things worthy of stripes, shall be beaten with few *stripes*. For unto whomsoever much is given, of him shall be much required: and to whom men have committed much, of him they will ask the more.**
>
> Luke 12:48

The more you know, the more is required. Sometimes you have it easy and do not even know it. Maybe God did not call you to know everything.

But now hath God set the members, every one of them in the body as it hath pleased HIM. But now are they many members, yet one body. The eye cannot say unto the hand, I have no need of you. Which do you think is more important, the eye or the hand? How can I say to you, I don't need you? I want to tell you something. I need you. I want you as God created you; I do not want you as the devil has re-created you. I'll meet you in your spiritual dynamics, but I need you whole. It would be better if you had an eye that could see, right?

So if I am going to have you, I would just as soon have you the way God created you. If you are the eye, then you need to be able to see. Then if God created you to be the foot, what do you need to be able to do? It doesn't do me any good if God created you to be the foot, and you don't go anywhere. You have to accept yourself as God has accepted you. So this stuff has to go.

The eye cannot say unto the hand, I have no need of you. Nor again the head to the feet, I have no need of you. Nay, much more those members of the body which seem to be more feeble... How many of you have said, well I am just feebleminded lately? How many of you have said, "I just don't have any strength; I am just feeble?" How many of you have felt less than important in the body lately? How many of you have felt like the body would not really miss you if you just kind of checked out? You need to be careful of self-unforgiveness, self-resentment, self-retaliation, self-anger, self-hatred, self-violence, because guess what comes next. Self-Murder. That is suicide. When you have suicide, you have self-bitterness and everything after it.

Do you want to learn how to deal with suicide cases? They are all over the place. Do you want to be able to deal with them? You have to break the Unloving spirit and get rid of the self-bitterness because self-hatred produces suicide. It says, "I need to eliminate myself, I do not belong here." That is an antichrist mentality. It is an antichrist thought, coming out of the armor of an Unloving spirit.

You do belong here. You have to accept the fact that you belong here. When God saved you, He said you belong here. Now when are you going to accept that fact? "Well, you don't know what my daddy told me when I was 13." Well, I know what God said about you before your daddy was ever conceived. Now what do you think about that? Read Psalm 139. Now who are you going to believe, your daddy in 1928 or God from the foundation of the world? Who are you going to believe? Whose report are you going to believe? Well, I am going to believe the report of the Lord.

Do you really want to be well? Do you really want to love yourself? Are you tired of this mess? Aren't you ready to get on with it? Then quit listening to lies. Lies are from an antichrist spirit because they contradict the Word of God about you! Not to believe the Word is rebellion!

Not Necessary

Those members of the body which seem to be more feeble, not necessary...

> Nay, much more those members of the body, which seem to be more feeble, are necessary: 1 Corinthians 12:22

"Oh, I am not too important. I am just the feeble one." There is a personality that calls itself no-name or the vacant one or the nonexistent one. "Do you exist?" "Nope." "Well, who is talking to me?" "No one." "What is your name?" "I do not have one; I am no-name." "Why do you have no name?" "Because I am not important. I don't exist. I don't matter." Are you hearing voices? Yes.

"Not necessary" is part of the armor. "I am not necessary. I am not important. I am not needed." That is part of the Unloving profile. Do you identify with this? "I am not important. I am not needed. I am not necessary. Life could go on without me, and no one would notice that I am missing." I would know you were missing, and God would know you were missing. Who are you fooling? Don't go on with your life and not feel important, because you are.

You are incredibly important to the whole picture, if you could just get hold of that. I want to tell you who has been ripped off. God has been ripped off by the devil. He is not too happy. What makes God happy is you, because you have been created for His pleasure. I ask you continually in ministry, "Who are you? Where did you come from? What is your name? Why are you here? I want to know who you are!" So do not tell me you came from the devil because that is not true. Even the devil came from God. Jesus created Lucifer.

Be who God created you to be! In ministry we give you back to God the way He wanted you from the beginning. Will you please show up and quit listening to lies and get on with it!? What does the Word say? All are important and all are necessary! "But you are such a failure." Do you know what I would say if I heard that voice? "Well, if I am, you have made me that way; God did not create me that way. If God did not create me that way, then you are messing with me. I am not the failure. You are the failure, and I agreed with you." You need to fall out of agreement with failure. You need to fall out of agreement with this failure-oriented mentality.

Jesus, the Word, really knows what He is saying here through Paul. Those members of the body that *"who"* thinks to be less honorable? God thinks or we think? Never look at one person and judge his value. The Word says if the judgment is coming about that person's value or importance, if it is a negative judgment, it is coming from other humans, even in the church. Do not judge people by their battle. Judge them by the faith of who they are in creation. Quit looking at what they are dressed up in.

If we judged you by the way you are right now, do you think we could minister healing and reconciliation to you? You must have faith to see beyond what is there. Where do you think that faith came from? We can look past the desolation to see what God created from the foundation of the world. He wants you to be the way He intended.

Do you think you need to die to become part of the body of Christ? You have to stand up and take your place in the land of the living once and for all. When the Son of man comes, will He find faith in the earth?

> **I tell you that he will avenge them speedily. Nevertheless when the Son of man cometh, shall he find faith on the earth?** Luke 18:8

Do you have faith to believe for yourself? The Unloving spirit won't let you do that because part of the armor of the Unloving spirit is unbelief and doubt. Self-Doubt and self-unbelief. That is tied to Fear and also to the Unloving spirit.

First Corinthians 12:23-24 says "Those members of the body which we think to be less honorable, upon these we bestow more abundant honor, and the uncomely parts had more abundant comeliness. For our comely parts have no need, but God hath tempered the body together having given more abundant honor to that part which lacked."

228

Do you know what has been really interesting to watch in the church? To see God raise up those we consider to be insignificant human beings, desolated and devastated by life, and make them some of the greatest warriors for the kingdom of God that mankind has ever seen. They are leaving all the PhD's standing behind in the dust, reading their Torahs every Sabbath. Meanwhile some insignificant, unlearned individual comes along, untempered, unqualified, unnecessary, anointed by God, accepted by God, and stands up in that love. They will tear the devil apart in power. Never discount yourself in any area of your life. It is time for you to take your place in the land of the living – in the body of Christ. You are important! God needs you because you are part of His corporate body in the earth.

Division

Scripture says,

That there should be no schism in the body;

1 Corinthians 12:25

Schism equals division. Part of an Unloving spirit's armor is division. An Unloving spirit won't allow you to flow with other people. It will divide and conquer. It will find other spirits just like itself to group around to divide and conquer. It is not interested in unity; it is interested in division. People who have an Unloving spirit that is ruling are not interested in peace; they are interested in war. They are interested in unloveliness being promoted. When there is schism and division, there is strife, and when there is strife, there is every evil thing. An Unloving spirit is able to propagate itself continually over and over and over again.

For our comely parts have no need, but God hath tempered the body together, having given more abundant honor to that part which lacks. For there shall be no schism in the body, but that the members shall have the same care one for another. Whether one member suffer, all the members suffer with it and when one member be honored, all the members rejoice with it. Now ye are the body of Christ and members in particular. God has set some in the church. First apostles, second prophets, thirdly teachers, after that miracles, then gifts of healing, helps, governments and diversity of tongues. In one verse, in one body, God has set a range from the greatest apostle to an individual member in the ministry of helps.

When you are hurting, we feel it. We feel just as hopeless as you do. We feel pain as you do. We feel everything that you feel, just maybe not exactly the same. We identify, we grieve, and we hurt because when one member of the body hurts, we all hurt! We need you.

There is a range from apostles to those serving in the ministry of helps. First Corinthians 12:29-31 asks: Are all apostles? No. Are all prophets? No. Are all workers of miracles? No. Have all the gifts of healing? No. Do all speak with tongues? No. Do all interpret? No. But covet earnestly the best gift and yet I show unto you *a more excellent way.* That is love. There is no place for an Unloving spirit where there is love.

We need to offer ourselves first as a gift because we are part of the body. The gifts are not for the edification of the person who has the gift, but for the body. When you study the gifts of the Holy Spirit in 1 Corinthians 12, they are not for the people who operate in the gifts of the Holy Spirit. Those gifts are for edification of the body. So Paul is saying, desire the best gift, we need you. The body needs you. So whatever you are and whatever God has placed you in the body to be, earnestly position yourself in a place that you could be used of God, not for yourself, because when the giftings come, it is a lot of work. To covet the best gift would be the very best God has for you in the body, and you need to be available for that end.

When someone gives you a testimony of healing, what is the first thing that shows up? Unbelief and doubt. Whenever you have good news, you always have the pessimist. "Well, I would not get my hopes built up too high..."

SPIRIT WORLD REALITIES

Carl Jung had an interest in what is called primitive, primate thinking in which he considered the pre-Christian era to be the source of all being. His focus was on communicating with the dead. He spent much time in trances and in all kinds of methods to communicate with the underworld of the dead. In fact, he considered himself a reincarnation of the god Mithras, and he was in communication with that entity. The archetypes and dark shadows are the devils. Actually Carl Jung was in contact with disembodied beings of the dead from before the Ice Age. They are the disembodied spirits, the souls of those beings that fell with Lucifer and the fallen angels that became the web of principalities and powers and the rulers of the darkness of this world and spiritual wickedness in high places.

Let's just get it really straight. When you die to self, what are you dying to? What is the flesh? What is sin? Where did it come from? Where is it today? What is it doing?

Editor's Note: Refer to *Spirit World Realities* for more information.

Dying to self is really you being liberated from self. What part of yourself do you want to be liberated from? Jesus said He came that you might have life and have it more abundantly. Do you think you should be the walking dead? Would you rather be walking around here as a dead person, or are you happy to be alive? In fact, one of the promises of the Word in Romans is the greatest hope we have.

> ¹⁹For the earnest expectation of the creature waiteth for the manifestation of the sons of God.
> ²⁰For the creature was made subject to vanity, not willingly, but by reason of him who hath subjected *the same* in hope,
> ²¹Because the creature itself also shall be delivered from the bondage of corruption into the glorious liberty of the children of God.
> ²²For we know that the whole creation groaneth and travaileth in pain together until now.
> ²³And not only *they*, but ourselves also, which have the firstfruits of the Spirit, even we ourselves groan within ourselves, waiting for the adoption, *to wit*, the redemption of our body.   Romans 8:19-23

Wow! Do you know what that is saying? That is the hope and the promise that we are not the walking dead. We are the resurrected from the dead. We are the redeemed. Whether we live or whether we die, we are the Lord's.

> For whether we live, we live unto the Lord; and whether we die, we die unto the Lord: whether we live therefore, or die, we are the Lord's.   Romans 14:8

First Corinthians says,

> ⁵²In a moment, in the twinkling of an eye, at the last trump: for the trumpet shall sound, and the dead shall be raised incorruptible, and we shall be changed.
> ⁵³For this corruptible must put on incorruption, and this mortal *must* put on immortality.   1 Corinthians 15:52-53

Now which is better, walking around as a skeleton or walking around with a new body? One of the great promises of your future is eternal life as a being. Would you rather be trapped in the second heaven as a disembodied spirit, or would you like to be walking around in any dimension you want? Would you like to be an evil spirit? What a boring life!

No wonder they're in torment when they cannot manifest themselves. They do not have a body. They cannot go to heaven. They have no place of existence. They cannot drive a car. They cannot get married. They cannot have fun. They have no hope. They are full of Fear. In fact they screamed out at Jesus, "Have you come to torment us before our time?" What a pitiful existence! Do we want to become one with that? With friends like them who needs enemies? One of the things that needs to be taught accurately in the Christian church is what we call Spirit World Realities.

Paul said very clearly in Romans 7 that when he wanted to do good, he could not, and when he did evil, he did not want to do it. It was no longer him that was doing the evil, but sin that dwelt within him was doing it — "the old man." He said he saw in his members that the law of sin was warring against the law of his mind, and bringing him into captivity to the law of sin in his members.

> ¹⁹For the good that I would I do not: but the evil which I would not, that I do.
> ²⁰Now if I do that I would not, it is no more I that do it, but sin that dwelleth in me.
> ²¹I find then a law, that, when I would do good, evil is present with me.
> ²²For I delight in the law of God after the inward man:
> ²³But I see another law in my members, warring against the law of my mind, and bringing me into captivity to the law of sin which is in my members.   Romans 7:19-23

One of the dangerous things about psychotherapy is that it does not involve casting out evil spirits. It uses integration. Do you really want to come in contact with them, cohabit with these things and be integrated with them; becoming one with them? If you say, "Well, if you do not like me, too bad. That is just the way I am. If God wanted me to be different, He would have created me differently. I was created the way I am, and so that is just the way I am."

233

Who said God created you the way you are right now? No, He did not create the evil. In Isaiah 14 is a key about Lucifer; it says iniquity was found within his heart. Did he have a devil? No. He made a choice in the spiritual dimension that involved rebellion against the living God, coming out of self-exaltation and self-idolatry. Then he led one-third of all angels in rebellion against God, and he took this planet and every being that lived here right down the tube. Then this planet was judged, as it says starting in Jeremiah 4:23, and the earth became without form and void.

> I beheld the earth, and, lo, *it was* without form, and void; and the heavens, and they had no light. Jeremiah 4:23

At that stage every being that was on this planet was judged in that climactic, incredible, cataclysmic event that produced the condition of being without form and void. Those beings were the epitome of a perverted nature. The Bible says the evil was beyond comprehension. God had to judge it because there was no one that cared about goodness anymore. Not even the leadership. Not even Lucifer. Not even the angels. No one wanted to be good. It was a horror scene.

Do you know where you can dip into that horror today? Just watch movies at the theater for a few days. Buy some videos, and you will see the same horror being re-created by Hollywood. Where do you think they learned how to speculate about that kind of horror? From muses and evil spirits. The Bible says there is nothing new under the sun.

In Genesis and also in Jude, the Bible says that evil spirits are angels that are reserved in chains of darkness awaiting judgment because they left their proper state of habitation. They willed to leave. Here is something you must understand: from angels to fallen beings, to you, all are freewill agents. You have been created by God to make quality decisions. No created being was ever created to be a puppet or a clone or to be a vegetable from the standpoint of spiritual intellect. You are fully capable of coming to conclusions. That is what is so important about the scriptures back in Joshua. The scriptures tell you to choose life or death, blessings or cursings.

> And if it seem evil unto you to serve the LORD, choose you this day whom ye will serve; whether the gods which your fathers served that *were* on the other side of the flood, or the gods of the Amorites, in whose land ye dwell: but as for me and my house, we will serve the LORD.   Joshua 24:15

> I call heaven and earth to record this day against you, *that* I have set before you life and death, blessing and cursing: therefore choose life, that both thou and thy seed may live:
> Deuteronomy 30:19

Every created being has the ability to make a choice. Did Jesus make a choice? He said, Father if it be possible take this cup from me, nevertheless, not my will, but thy will be done. What is the choice? Why do I serve God today, why do you serve God? *Because you choose to.* You are making a quality decision.

Lucifer sinned when there was no reason to sin, and you choose not to sin when you have every reason to. If you blow it, you make another quality decision to repent and take responsibility. That is a choice. Every created being is capable of being Luciferian, including you and me. That is why mankind is on probation. God is trying the reins of your heart because any one of us could become another Lucifer. Any of us could become like a fallen angel and potentially become reprobate in our heart and rebellious against God. Those angels were tempted with self-exaltation, power, supremacy, rulership, leadership. Why? Because God created us to rule. Are you tempted to be a king and a priest now? You have been called to be a ruler.

Because they know they are called to be rulers, many people in the Christian church try to get ahead of it and want to become rulers now. They try to create their own kingdoms, their own rulership, on their own basis. You have been created to rule. You have been created to have dominion over the earth. The possibility of any created being sinning is always there and will always be there eternally.

What is the key? When King David was confronted with his issues, what did he do? In Psalm 51 he came before God, and now all of a sudden he is called a man after God's own heart. Why? It was not because he could not fall, because he did fall. It was because he repented.

Lucifer never repented and neither did the Unloving spirits. One-third of all angels never did either. What sets us apart from that dimension is having a humble and a contrite heart and taking responsibility when we fall short of the glory of the living God in creation. That is what separates the sons of God from the sons of the devil. That is what separates the sons of light from the sons of darkness. That is the difference.

What made David a man after God's own heart? Two things: he loved God, and he took responsibility for sin. Not at first, but eventually. What is the key for you then, to be a man or woman after God's own heart? Love God, and take responsibility for your failures. Be honest and say, "I blew it."

False piety is rooted in a religious spirit. Piety means duty to God, devotion to religious duties and practices, loyalty and devotion to parents and family. A pious act, statement of belief. I will give you a good definition of false piety. This will cut through some issues. I hope you don't stone me. "Well, pastor I know that my parents abused me, victimized me, rejected me, but haven't you heard in the

Word to honor your father and mother? So I am just going to have to submit to this; I am just going to have to go back into it." That is false piety.

Nowhere in the Word does it teach that we submit to evil. When it says to honor your father and mother, that means to do so if they are honoring God themselves. It does not mean to be swallowed up by their evil spiritual dynamics. I do not believe you need to honor a mother and a father if they are ungodly. You do not have to come back at them in war and destroy them, but you do not have to submit to evil.

God has called us to peace. If the Bible says you are to have a perfect hatred for evil, why would you submit to evil? So false piety has a religious spirit attached to it because it produces martyrdom. There is true martyrdom, and there is false martyrdom. Have you ever seen a false martyr? "Well, I'll just have to take it; it is God's lot for my life."

I tried to minister to a guy one time that had extreme pain. I said, "Well, you know the Lord can heal you of that. Would you like me to pray for you?" "Oh, no brother," he said. "This pain is mine to endure. It reminds me of the sufferings of Christ at the cross and every day this pain sears my body. I am just so in love with God because it reminds me of His pain for me."

What was that? False piety. "Well, Pastor, my sufferings allow me to identify with the pain of the world." What is that? False piety. "Well, it's my lot in life, besides someone has to be the doormat. Well, haven't you heard, Pastor, that you are to prefer another over yourself? So I'm a 'nobody', and I just let everyone else take the preeminence." What is that? False piety. That is an Unloving spirit. That is not what

Psalm 139 says. It says you are "fearfully and wonderfully made." The hand of God is upon you!

Let's go to the word "self" in the dictionary. There are two parts to self. We have to go back to Romans 7 again in our thinking. Paul said there was a part of him that was good; but there were two parts of him. He said, I know that in me, that is in my flesh dwelleth no good thing. That would be his nature, his carnal nature. For to will is present with me. "To will" means to make a quality choice. For to will is present with me, but how to perform that which is good I find not. For the good that I would, I do not do it. The evil which I would not, that is what I do. Now if I do those things I wish I would not, it is no more I that do it, but sin that dwelleth in me. I find then a law that when I would do good, evil is present with me. Are both these parts, parts of his self? Paul is saying that he saw partly good and partly evil in himself. That is exactly what he was saying.

What is a law? Romans 7 says that when I do these evil things, I consent unto the law that the evil that I am doing is good. I consent unto the law that it is good. Then it says, but I find then a law that when I would do good, evil is present with me. What Paul is saying is that there are two laws working within him. What does the word "law" mean? Precepts. Concepts. The Word of God.

What he is saying is that within me are two opposing veins of thinking. This part over here loves God. Amen. Hallelujah, I am a son of God. Over here is this law within me that is bringing another word, another concept, another idea, another suggestion to get me to follow it. So when I follow the law of evil, I say to the law of God, "You are bad," and I say to the law of evil, "You are good." Both laws establish a code of thought, word and deed. Both codes promote a mechanism of thought, word and deed. So in deed, what do you do? You follow one or the other. Are you following the law of God? Or are you following the law of anti-God?

One of the things about Carl Jung is that he promoted another gospel, the gospel of anti-God. In fact some of the material that I am reading about him says he wanted to give God back to Himself. God had gotten lost, and so we needed to find God, not for our sake, but for God's sake. So he wanted to create a gospel that was anti-God so that God could find Himself outside the parameters of the gospel. That is a slight twist, a law within. A statement of direction, a statement of thinking.

Paul says I find then a law that when I would do good, evil is present with me, for I delight in the law of God after the inward man. Is that part of him? But there is another part of himself he talks about when he says he sees another law in his members. It is warring against the law of his mind and bringing him into captivity to the law of sin, which is in his members. Wow! This is Psychology 101 and you did not even know it. This is the true insight, not the pagan one. I am going to find Paul one day when I get to heaven, and I am going to give that boy a big hug because this is the antidote to psychology. This is the truth of a man who struggled with two kingdoms — the kingdom of God and the kingdom of sin. He gave an honest statement about both kingdoms working in us.

Now, let's go back and read the word "self" in the dictionary. Self is a noun, and then it comes as a prefix with a dash, like Self-Pity, self-rejection. Let's go back and read the word "self." In Middle English, the word means separate, apart. Have you heard the scripture that says that your souls shall be saved? First Corinthians 5:5 says that Paul gave someone over to Satan for the destruction of the flesh so that the spirit may be saved in the day of judgment. So you have your soul being saved, and you have your spirit being saved — the whole reality of salvation spiritually includes your spirit and your soul. Now right here it says in the word self, by itself, separate. So when you say "self," that means first of all that you are a separate unique identity. I am separately and uniquely different, and I stand alone as an individual. That is part of my composition. That is part of who I am, my identity.

God said in Psalm 139:14 that you, you personally, are fearfully and wonderfully made. Before you were ever conceived, God saw your parts and your pieces as they were curiously wrought in the bowels of the earth, out of the dust of the earth. He fashioned them in His mind and His creative ability and the genetics of your ancestry from Adam and Eve, and He saw you before you ever came, uniquely individual, uniquely separate. So separate, that your name is written down in heaven.

Would you say that indicates that you are a separate entity? In that day you shall be known as you are known. Identity is part of your self and when your soul is saved, your identity is saved and your spiritual dynamics are saved. Do you think that when we get to heaven, we will remember that David had Uriah killed? Will we remember that Peter denied the Lord? It is written down.

Who are you? Are you a split personality? Are you a multiple personality? Are you a fabricated personality? Who are you? Self. "Well, I do not really exist. I am fabricated into 14 or 15 or 16 different entities." "Well, would the real one please stand up?" "There is none." "Wrong. There is one. It is that person found in Psalm 139 that says you are fearfully and wonderfully made and the hand of God is upon you. It is that one from the foundation of the world."

Paul said from the foundation of the world God ordained that he be an apostle to the Gentiles. God said to Jeremiah, "Before you were ever conceived, I ordained you to be a prophet to the nations." That is self-identity, knowing your identity.

This Unloving spirit is banking on the fact that, with his armor, you will never be who you were created to be. He is banking on the fact that it is a law screaming in your ears day and night about who you really are. Well, whose law are you going to remember, and whose law are you going to follow? Will you believe this law screaming in your head of Self-Pity, self-rejection, competition, self-pride, self-enthronement, false piety, "I" and "I will," self-exaltation, attention getting, excessive talkativeness, insecurity, self-mutilation, excessive eating and bingeing, self-comparison, self-idolatry, perfectionism, self-torment, defending oneself, self-doubt, unbelief, self-bitterness, self-resentment, self-unforgiveness, self-retaliation, self-anger, self-hatred, self-violence and suicide? When all of that is screaming in your head and you are listening to it, you are saying to the law of God that it is a lie! According to your faith, so be it. That stuff has to go.

I am not going to stand before the Lord in heaven and say, "Well, Lord, I know I am fearfully and wonderfully made. I know I am the apple of Your eye. I know You love me with an everlasting love. I know I am the righteousness of God through Christ Jesus by faith. I know I am a son (or a daughter) of God. I know I am a king and a priest. I know You said that." He'll look at you and say, "Then why did you waste your time walking in this part of yourself that came from hell and the devil? Why did you do that when you had My Word? Why did you call me a liar when I said I loved you?" Whose report will you believe? I shall believe the report of the Lord. Let God be true and every man and devil and angel and created being that would preach another gospel be accursed and be a liar. The Holy Spirit is telling you the truth every single minute of the day if you will listen. There is another law warring against the law of your mind, in your spirit and in your mind, demanding that you follow that gospel of self.

The first definition of "self" in the dictionary is "the identity, the character or essential qualities of any person or thing." The second definition is "one's own person as distinct from all others, one's own welfare, interest or advantage, selfishness, obsessed with self, myself, himself, herself, yourself, of the same kind, nature, color, material as the rest, the self-lining, the self-trim." These are all the definitions of self.

When you crucify the flesh, you crucify the old nature of Satan within you. Everything that you are, you have been programmed either by your life circumstances or you inherited familiar spirits from your ancestry that made you start thinking that way right from birth. The spirit of Rejection can be found right in the womb. What do you think is meant by scriptures like Proverbs 22:15 that say evil or foolishness is bound up in the heart of a child? The child inherited the familiar spirits that produce that evil.

Who are you? What are your characteristics? What is meant to "put on Christ?" What is meant to "be created in His image?" What is meant to be "created in the image of God?" What is meant to be "uniquely different yet uniquely one with God in His nature?" Self.

Another definition of "self" is "of oneself or itself." This refers to the direct object of the implied transitive verb such as self-love, self-restraint. These are the faculties of the Holy Spirit. Do you know you can have self-making decisions? Is temperance an act of self? Is longsuffering an act of self? Is love an act of self? Is patience an act of self? Is forgiveness an act of self? These are actions that you are taking. You are expressing who you are according to your nature. Your spiritual nature, and your soul should become one with the attributes of God in creation.

When you are split, you are not that way. You are half, "I need to be loved," and half, "I don't want to be loved." Then you wonder why you are in torment. One half of you is screaming out because God created you to be loved, because He is love. He created you with the ability to be able to give and receive love.

So in your creation, inside yourself you are saying, "I need to be loved." This voice says, "No one loves me. But I need to be loved." Then if someone comes up and says, "I love you," you say, "No you don't. Leave me alone. You don't mean it. You're not sincere. You have always lied to me. You are just like the rest of them. Get away from me." Inside of you, it is saying, "I need to be loved. Why did I say that?" Then comes the guilt, then comes the hatred, then comes the Bitterness, and you are caught in this web of double mindedness. "I need to be loved. I don't want to be loved." You wonder why you are having a bad day. That is confusion.

Well, would you finally make up your mind what you want? Do you want to be loved or not? If you do, receive it. The Unloving spirit won't let you receive it. Receive it anyway, and quit being double minded. Quit listening to the other law warring in your members, warring against the law of your mind and bringing you into captivity to law of sin, which is self-hatred.

The Bible says to "put on" and "put off." Do a word study on "put off" and "put on." Put away your idols. Put away your images. Put on the garment of praise. Put off the

243

spirit of heaviness. Put on, put off... What you are putting on, and what are you putting off will determine who you really are. Do you want your personality to be formed by evil spirits? Do you want to be half holy and half evil all your life? Do not listen to that lie! It is another law. God loves you!

Another definition of "self" is "self-abasement," which means you are living in a basement by yourself. That is the prison house we are talking about in Luke 11. You are down in the basement, and the strong man is sitting up in your easy chair in your living room. You are down there in that basement, down there in your self-abasement lifestyle.

The armor comes with feelings and emotions and thoughts. These all come with sights, sounds and smells. They all come with a video. They all come with words. They all come with feelings. They all come with emotions. They all come bringing a reality within you. You cannot think of Self-Bitterness without experiencing it. You feel it.

Self-Abnegation, Self-Absorption, Self-Introspection

Self-Abnegation means lack of consideration for oneself or one's own interest, self-denial. Do you know how many people go into denial concerning themselves? Self-Absorption would almost be equivalent to self-introspection. Self-Absorption means being absorbed in one's own interests and affairs. Many people are so tied up in themselves. They can't see the forest because of the trees. They are so wrapped up in their stuff, they can't even see past it. Many people believe they cannot be healed, not just because of unbelief and doubt, but because of self-absorption and self-introspection.

Self-Abuse

Self-Abuse is misuse of one's own abilities, talents. It includes self-accusation. Self-Abuse includes self-blame, self-revilement, self-acting, and self-advancement, which is the act of advancing or promoting one's own interest. It includes self-aggrandizement, which is the act of making oneself more powerful and wealthy, especially in a ruthless way. It is also self-analysis, which is the analysis of one's own personality without the help of another.

Self-Annihilation is loss of awareness of self, as in a mystical union with God. It means becoming "the vacant one." It means totally removing yourself as a person. That is heresy and that is an inaccuracy. I want to tell you something, God wants you to become more aware of yourself, but with God at the center. God wants you to become more aware. Hebrews 5:14 says that one who is able to handle strong meat is one who by reason of exercise of his senses is able to discern good and evil. Paul also said that he served God with the inner man.

> **That he would grant you, according to the riches of his glory, to be strengthened with might by his Spirit in the inner man;** Ephesians 3:16

Self-Denial

When you go into self-denial and remove yourself, you eliminate or deny yourself from who you really are. "Out of sight, out of mind" is not a spiritual principle. Many people say, "I do not want to talk about that because it just stirs up too much in me, so I'll just suppress it." Suppression is a form of bondage because then you are just allowing that thing to torment you without you thinking about it. If something is going to torment me, I would like to know about it. I mean if I am going to have an enemy here and someone is going to torment me, I would like to know.

245

Self-Annihilation

Self-Annihilation is a loss of awareness of oneself. That sets the stage up for suicide. As a spirit of death, it eliminates your value and is contradictory to Psalm 139 that says you are fearfully and wonderfully made and that the hand of God is upon you. Self-Annihilation is an antichrist mentality.

Say this, "I have the right to exist. I am ordained by God to be here. God came to save me, not to get rid of me."

We are kings and priests in the making. We are coming back as kings and priests. Zechariah says,

> ¹Behold, the day of the LORD cometh, and thy spoil shall be divided in the midst of thee.
> ²For I will gather all nations against Jerusalem to battle; and the city shall be taken, and the houses rifled, and the women ravished; and half of the city shall go forth into captivity, and the residue of the people shall not be cut off from the city.
> ³Then shall the LORD go forth, and fight against those nations, as when he fought in the day of battle.
> ⁴And his feet shall stand in that day upon the mount of Olives, which *is* before Jerusalem on the east, and the mount of Olives shall cleave in the midst thereof toward the east and toward the west, *and there shall be* a very great valley; and half of the mountain shall remove toward the north, and half of it toward the south.
> ⁵And ye shall flee *to* the valley of the mountains; for the valley of the mountains shall reach unto Azal: yea, ye shall flee, like as ye fled from before the earthquake in the days of Uzziah king of Judah: and the LORD my God shall come, *and* all the saints with thee.　　　Zechariah 14:1-5

The total purpose of God through Jesus Christ is to save your soul and your spirit and to give you a new body in the resurrection. That is the teaching of the gospel. God wants you to be preserved without this junk in you. Do you want to be the real you? That old Unloving spirit says you need to be eliminated. God, who is love, says that you are loved and accepted and that He needs you.

Say, "Self-Annihilation, get out of here. God needs me." Amen.

Self-Appointed, Self-Assertion

Self-Appointed and self-assertion both remove God's ordination. Romans 8:14 tells us that those "who are led by the Spirit of God are the sons of God." When people "self-assert," moving themselves into places and positions, sometimes that is coming out of an Unloving spirit. Self-Assertion is the act of demanding recognition for oneself or of insisting upon one's rights and claims. That is a very, very dangerous situation.

Self-Assurance, Self-Awareness, Self-Centeredness

Self-Assurance, self-awareness, and being self-centered are very dangerous. The Unloving spirit is very self-centered. Self-Centered means being occupied or concerned only with one's own affairs. It is egocentric and selfish. Self-Centeredness is very dangerous because it eliminates you as a gift or a servant. Self-Centeredness always wants to be served, but a servant always serves. We are trying to give you back your identity, not to make you self-centered. We want to free you.

There is a type of self-centeredness in which "me, myself and I" is very dangerous and influenced by evil spirits. There is another part where you are released to be a gift, as God saw you from the foundation of the world.

Self-Piety

How do you draw the line between self-centeredness and self-piety? First of all, self-centeredness revolves around self-preservation, and self-piety centers around false humility. It is a way to establish a value when you do not feel you have any value. There is that self-exaltation, attention getting and perfectionism. God wants you to look inward, but He does not want you to become preoccupied with yourself because when you are, you will want to be served. What can someone do for me today? No, it is what you can do for someone today.

Remember the fast you are called to in Isaiah 58. The fast God has called you to is that of service, and then will your health spring forth speedily. The bonds of wickedness will be broken.

When you are bound by an Unloving spirit it is very difficult to serve anyone, because you are self-serving.

You can help someone else and not be totally healed yourself.

Helping others is the beginning of your healing. You are pouring the life of God into the sick, and the very thing you are pouring into them is what you are receiving.

Self-Consciousness

Self-Consciousness is coming out of an Unloving spirit. Self-Consciousness is self-awareness and self-introspection. When you are self-conscious of yourself, you are actually comparing yourself to others. It is coming out of a lack of self-approval. There is an element of Fear to self-consciousness. It is rooted in Fear of rejection, Fear of man and Fear of failure. Remember that Fear and the Unloving spirit link arms and hang out together. Self-Consciousness is part of the Unloving profile, but it brings with it Fear of man. Being unduly conscious of oneself when noticed by others and being awkward or embarrassed in the presence of others is Fear. Having or showing an awareness of one's own existence, actions, conscious of oneself, one's ego, self-conscious comes from Fear linking with Unloving.

Self-Deception

Self-Deception, creating your own delusional realities, is also very dangerous. Self-Deception is deceiving oneself to one's true feelings, motives and circumstances.

Self-Effacement

Self-Effacement is the practice of keeping oneself in the background and minimizing one's own actions. It means modest, retiring behavior. Now that can be good to some degree, but under the Unloving spirit, it is not good. It is coming out of false piety and is a form of pride.

Self-Emulation, Self-Hatred

Self-Hatred is a hatred directed at oneself or one's own people, often in despair. Self-Emulation is suicide, usually by burning oneself in a public place. Why do people do that? To gain attention because they do not have any value system. It is their way of going out with a bang. The new form of suicide is to do something bizarre to get a policeman to shoot you. This creates a very dangerous public setting.

Self-Importance

Self-Importance means too much concern about one's own welfare.

Self-Love

Self-Love means "love of oneself, regard for oneself and one's own interest." Now there are two sides to self-love. It can be bad, too, but we are teaching how to love yourself with a right spirit. To give you an idea of the difference between lust and love, there is a wrong spirit behind one and a right spirit behind the other. Lust always takes. Love never takes. It only participates in what is given to it. What's the difference? One is taking, one is receiving.

Self-Pity

Self-Pity is pity for oneself, especially pity that is self-indulgent or exaggerated.

Self-Questioning

Self-Questioning means always doubting one's own beliefs and motives. It means not having any confidence in oneself. It means no self-confidence, self-doubt.

Self-Reproach

Self-Reproach is Accusation or blame of oneself. It involves feelings of guilt and includes self-accusation.

Guilt

Guilt is a form of condemnation. Guilt is very much a part of the Unloving spirit. Self-Guilt is not being able to forgive oneself and includes self-unforgiveness. Self-Unforgiveness and self-resentment produce guilt, and all of the Bitterness underlings produce guilt.

Self-Torture, Self-Mutilation

Self-Torture and self-mutilation include mental and physical distress. Self-Mutilation can be caused by mental distress. You can really do yourself in. Fear has torment. Those phobic realities and those nightmares come out of a Fear of torture. Self-Torture, mental torture, horror and self-torment are all part of mental torment.

Dying to self does not mean we are eliminating ourselves. Dying to self is putting to death the old man, and removing the spirits that are creating this personality within you. Either they are present or they have programmed you in your memes or your memory banks.

Self-Indulgence, Kleptomania

Kleptomania is shoplifting. People who shoplift have the need for a fix, and it is rooted in an Unloving spirit. All

250

kleptomania is rooted in the need to be self-indulged. People who shoplift are desperately trying to be caught. Now some people who steal are just thieves, but kleptomaniacs are not thieves. They do not need it for substance or to survive. They need to steal in order to fill an inner void. They really don't even know it, but they want to be caught for attention. But when they get that kind of attention, it brings more guilt, more Self-Hatred and reinforces the Unloving spirit.

Compulsive Spending, Bingeing

A person who compulsively spends money needs that rush and that fix because they do not feel good about themselves. Compulsive spending, like bingeing, is to satisfy that craving for something and is built right into the Unloving spirit. It is built right into the lack of serotonin. It is built into the thoughts you have — that you are not feeling good, that you are not accepted, that you are not a whole person, and that you are not loved. You need that fix.

It's a vicious circle. It's the same thing as taking cocaine. Cocaine addiction is a psychologically addictive disease, not a chemically addictive disease, because it releases massive amounts of dopamine, the pleasure neurotransmitter. When people take a hit of cocaine, they never get the same rush ever again, and they try so hard to do it. Dopamine is not remanufactured by the body quickly. If you are continually using cocaine, you are continually depleting dopamine. This addiction could be caused by a spirit that never allows you to be satisfied, but drives you. If you have depleted serotonin levels, you need a fix to feel good about yourself. An Unloving spirit of self-rejection and self-hatred causes depleted serotonin levels.

Environmental Illness

Environmental Illness is a "self" disease. Self-Pity must be broken because it binds you to the past and won't release you from the spiritual dynamics of your past. It keeps you from the provision of God for your future. It binds you to what you have done and what someone else has done. It tells you that no one really understands, and people do not really care. If they did care, they would love you more. They would sit on your doorstep. They would call you every day. They would not ignore you. They would do this, or they would do that. But when a person finally comes and sits on your doorstep every day, you tell him to go away because you are unloved, you do not want him around anyway, and now he is bugging you.

That is the mechanism of Self-Pity. Self-Pity is very dangerous, because it will never, never allow you to be free. I have not found one person totally healed of MCS/EI since 1990 who did not get this dealt with. I have not found one person totally healed of MCS/EI in America who did not get the Unloving spirit dealt with, because that is what causes it. It is comprised of a broken heart, Fear, Fear of rejection, Fear of man, Fear of failure, Fear of not being loved, Self-Pity. MCS/EI is a self-disease because it stands on two legs, and one is Fear.

Fear is a form of faith. It creates introspection. Fear says you won't survive. An Unloving spirit comes along and says you don't need to. You're not important anyway. Your body is responding to a mixture of oppression. Remember the book of Proverbs says,

> **A merry heart doeth good** *like* **a medicine: but a broken spirit drieth the bones.**   Proverbs 17:22

When your system gets compromised, allergies come and now you have become preoccupied with self. MCS/EI is a preoccupation with self because the entire profile of MCS/EI involves phobias, and phobic realities which involve projection and displacement or avoidance. So your whole day is now around self. What am I going to avoid? Do they
252

have perfume on? What's going on? What am I eating? What's here? What's there? Your whole day is caught up in projecting and then avoiding what you are projecting. Your whole life is now wrapped up in self-preservation from reactions and other diseases. Then all of a sudden these ten or twelve diseases come along; candida, hypothyroidism, fibromyalgia and all these other peripheral diseases come. Now you really have something to think about. Now you have 14 specialists you can go and listen to. Now you are obsessed with self-preservation.

Self-Sabotage

Self-Sabotage is really rooted in the Unloving spirit. It is tied closely with self-mutilation and self-destruction and is very dangerous. Self-Sabotage will destroy your faith, because faith is the substance of things hoped for, the evidence not yet seen. Self-Sabotage says your faith will never work for you, and if it tries to work, it needs to be destroyed. In other words, self-sabotage will keep you from ever achieving any hopes. Proverbs 13:12 says, "Hope deferred maketh the heart sick." Now you're caught in a very vicious web of a sick heart and a sick mind, still needing to be loved and still needing to overcome. There is a spirit now that says you do not qualify, and everything good that happens to you needs to be destroyed. That reinforces the Unloving spirit within you.

Self-Sabotage is very prevalent. You are not able to receive anything good, first of all. Second of all, you think God is punishing you. It is setting yourself up so you never go ahead and try to do anything because you know that you are going to destroy it, or something within you is going to destroy it. We call that a curse. "Wasted years and a wasted life" comes out of self-sabotage. It is a fruit of an Unloving spirit. "Wasted years and a wasted life" is coming directly out of an Unloving spirit. It is self-hatred, self-rejection, self-destruction and the whole thing says, "I am never going to win. I am never going 'to be,' I do not need 'to be,' I am not going 'to be.' " If the wasted years start to turn around, self-sabotage will be destroyed.

One of the great tragedies of an Unloving spirit of self-sabotage is that people can have a great, great need to be loved. They get into a relationship, and the minute the other one says, "I love you and I care for you," this thing comes up in them. Everything goes downhill; it's self-sabotage from that point. There is an Unloving spirit that won't allow them to live in that love. They can't stand it. Love, what they need most, is what they end up destroying. That is extremely evil.

Would the real self please stand up? Who did God create and who are you? You cannot be healed of MCS/EI and hang onto an Unloving spirit, because that is what caused the disease to begin with. When your broken heart has been healed, you feel loved. Receiving God's love and loving yourself is the beginning of all freedom. It is only possible because of the Father, Jesus and the work of the Holy Spirit. It is not possible any other way. You cannot come to peace while staying in cohabitation with your archetypes (evil spirits). You can only be in peace when they are gone.

I am a son of God by faith. How about you? I am not led by my urges. I am led by the Word of God and the Spirit of God. How about you? I accept who I am in creation because I have that revelation from God as a work of the Holy Spirit, and Jesus came to show me and make it possible to the degree that He calls me a brother. That is a pretty close association, that the Lord calls me a brother. He is my Savior. He is my Creator. He is the second member of the Godhead, who created me from the foundation of the world, who has saved me and redeemed me. He is my Lord. He is my *Adon*. He is the Bishop of my soul. He is my King. He is my God, but He is also my brother. Wow! To top it off, *Adonay Yhovih* is my Father. I never had it so good in all my life!

Do you want the Unloving spirit broken?

Fellowship with the Godhead is a beginning. When you have your completeness in fellowship with the Godhead, you will love yourself, and these characters won't have a shot at you. What is the worst thing that can happen to you? You can die, go to heaven and come back again.

Are you ready to get rid of these critters? We are going to go before the Lord and ask Him to free us. We are going to ask Him for the power of the devil to be broken. If you have the same thoughts as before, the minute we finish, do not go into unbelief and doubt. This is a battle for your life. Not only do you have the spirits that need to be dealt with and put under authority, but your mind needs to be renewed by a practical application every day of your freedom.

One of the things we learned about EI is that a Walk Out time is needed. A lot of people are so busy trying "in the name of Jesus to be healed," and "by His stripes you were healed," that they forget there is sometimes a battle still going on after the power of the devil is broken. There is still the process of your taking back your life and walking in freedom every day. Walk Out time is not a statement of unbelief; it is a statement of knowledge and wisdom. It puts the devil right back under your feet.

Pray this prayer with me (on the next page).

Father, I thank You for this day. I thank You for this teaching concerning the principality of the Unloving spirit. I thank You for the insight into how it links itself with Fear. Fear, we are going to deal with you very soon.

Father, I ask you to bring all things to my remembrance concerning this insight into the armor this principality uses to reinforce itself historically and personally in my life. I ask that my discernment would be acute, that my resolution to be free of this would be a constant part of my thinking, that You would be with me, and that You would prepare my heart to receive from You, in the name of Jesus. Amen.